ABSTRACT

The Social Worker in the Emergency Room
By
Dr. César M. Garcés Carranza

This study examined the perceptions that doctors and nurses hold of the role of the social worker in the emergency room and compares them with social workers' self-perceptions of what they actually do. The hypotheses of the study were: (1) Perceptions of social workers' roles in the medical emergency room will vary significantly by profession: Social Work, Medicine, and Nursing. (2) There will be no significant differences among doctors and nurses in their perceptions of social workers' roles in the emergency room by type of hospital (municipal and voluntary).

The sample consists of 117 emergency department social workers, doctors, and nurses employed in 20 New York City metropolitan hospitals (38 social workers, 39 doctors, and 40 nurses. The research instrument used to measure perceptions of social work practice in hospital emergency rooms was an adaptation of an instrument developed by Carrigan (1974), who explored the perceptions of interdisciplinary social work practice in two general medical/surgical Veterans Administration hospitals. It was modified for the study in order to make it relevant to the on-site experience of the respondents. The data were gathered using a questionnaire distributed to social workers, doctors, and nurses working in medical emergency rooms in two types of hospitals in New York City, municipal and voluntary (not-for profit). For profit hospitals were excluded from this study, because of the researcher's specific interest in municipal and voluntary hospitals. The data collected from the survey were analyzed using a statistical package for social services (**SPSS,** 1999). Pearson's Chi-Square was used to compute the difference, between observed and expected observations (responses) of the role of the social worker in the emergency room among social workers, doctors, and nurses. The hypotheses were tested in the Null form; the .05 or lower level of significance was used.

The overall findings demonstrate that social workers perceive their role in the emergency room as providers of clinical and concrete services. On the other hand, doctors and nurses perceive the role of the social worker as providers of concrete services. The literature reviewed since 1967 to 2000 shows that there have been no change in the way social workers are perceived by physicians, nurses, patients, and administrators in hospital settings. This study is different from Carrigan' s (1974) in that it examined the perceptions of the role of the social worker in the emergency room by doctors and nurses and compared them with social workers' self perceptions of what they do.

THE SOCIAL WORKER
IN THE
EMERGENCY ROOM

DR. CÉSAR M. GARCÉS CARRANZA

Inquiries and Book Orders should be addressed to:

Great Writers Media
Email: info@greatwritersmedia.com
Phone: 877-600-5469

Library of Congress Control Number: 2023903782

ISBN: 978-1-960605-26-9 (sc)
ISBN: 978-1-960605-27-6 (ebk)

The committee for this doctoral dissertation consists of:

Susan Mason, Ph.D., Chairperson, Wurzweiler School of Social Work, New York, NY Louis Levitt, D.S.W., Reader, Wurzweiler, School of Social Work, New York, NY Esther Chachkes, D. S.W., Reader, Social Work Director, NYU Medical Center, New York, NY

ACKNOWLEDGEMENTS

I wish to express my gratitude and deepest thanks to a number of people who made a unique contribution to this endeavor.

To my wife Ellen and our children Nicholas and Rachel whose belief in me and their unconditional support and patience gave me the strength to persevere and to prevail.

To my brothers and my sisters for their unconditional support and love. To my parents in law Ronald and Hellen Graeser who believed in me and gave me their unconditional support.

To friends and colleagues of Bronx Lebanon Hospital who gave me the fortitude to persevere and to prevail.

To Dr. Jean Atkatz who "opened the doors."

To Dr. Louis Levitt, former Director of the Doctoral Program for giving me the opportunity to reach my goal.

To Ms. Catherine Cassidy for her unconditional support.

My most profound gratitude and appreciation goes to Dr. Susan Mason. It is her wisdom. Guidance, steadfast encouragement, dedication and patience that made what was at first a dream. A reality.

I would like to thank the social workers, doctors, and nurses who participated in this study. Their responsiveness and willingness to take their time from their busy schedules in order to be involved, is appreciated.

DEDICATION

This dissertation is dedicated
to my parents Luis and Domitila

CONTENTS

Bronx Care Health System,
formally Bronx lebanon Hospital Center.

CHAPTER ONE

Dissertation Overview

Introduction

This study examines the perceptions that doctors and nurses hold of the role of the social worker in the emergency room and compares them with social workers' self perceptions of what they actually do. In addition, this study examines the relationship between types of hospitals, municipal vs. voluntary, and perceptions of social workers, doctors, and nurses about the role of the social worker. The study is descriptive, as defined by Rubin & Babbie (1997). The data consist of 117 medical emergency department social workers, doctors, and nurses employed in 20 New York City metropolitan hospitals.

The data were gathered using a questionnaire distributed to social workers, doctors, and nurses that work in the medical emergency room in two types of hospital in New York City, municipal and voluntary (not-for profit). For-profit hospitals were excluded from this study, because of the researcher's specific interest in municipal and voluntary hospitals. The participating hospitals were recruited from the 1998-1999 edition of the American Hospital Association Guide (American Hospital Association, 1961), which includes a list of all New York City acute care member hospitals. The hospitals for this study were selected on the basis of accessibility to the researcher. The sample consists of 38 social workers, 39 doctors, and 40 nurses.

The research instrument used here to measure perceptions of social work practice in hospital emergency rooms was an adaptation of an instrument developed by Carrigan (1974), who explored perceptions of interdisciplinary social work practice in two general medical/surgical Veteran's Administration hospitals. It was modified for the study in order to make it relevant to the on-site experience of the respondents.

In the original instrument, Carrigan (1974) examined factors that might affect professional perceptions of the social work role, such as the degree of contact with social workers or professional orientation to social work. This aspect of the instrument was kept intact. Several modifications were made in Carrigan's (1974) instrument for this study to increase ease of administration and validity. First, Carrigan began every item with "The social worker should." This construction was redundant and simply increased the length of the questionnaire. Therefore, the phrase, "The social worker should" was placed at the top of the list, and the rest of the item stem was included. This made the items and the questionnaire more easily readable.

A second modification was that the respondents limited the comparison with other persons. Instead, respondents focused on the extent to which the social worker should perform these functions. Respondents were asked to code their answers as follows:

1. **NEVER OR RARELY** done by social workers (about 5% of the time).
2. **SELDOM** done by social workers (about 25% of the time).
3. **SOMETIMES** done by social workers (about 50% of the time).
4. **OFTEN** done by social workers (about 75% of the time).
5. **ALWAYS OR NEARLY ALWAYS** done by social workers (about 95% of the time).

Carrigan's study was conducted in two Veteran's Administration hospitals associated with medical and social work schools. Her sample included 181 staff psychiatrists, psychologists, registered nurses, social workers, and administrators who were surveyed on their perceptions of the tasks that social workers actually perform. Carrigan (1974) concluded that the medical and nursing staff did not expect the social workers to perform highly skilled functions such as counseling or administrative services. The purpose of the present study is to replicate Carrigan's (1974) work and to add insights that pertain to municipal and voluntary hospitals in a large metropolitan area.

The data collected from the survey were analyzed using a statistical software package for social services, SPSS version (SPSS, 1999). Pearson's Chi-Square was used to compute the differences between observed and expected observations (responses) of the role of the social worker in the emergency room among social workers, doctors, and nurses. Pearson's Chi-Square is a powerful statistical tool that assumes that the data are measured at the nominal and ordinal level (Rubin & Babbie, 1997). The hypotheses were tested in the null form; the .05 or lower level of significance was used.

Current studies show that doctors and nurses in hospital settings most frequently refer patients for social work intervention when there is a need for concrete services, such as providing transportation or making telephone calls (Auslander & Schneidman, 1996; Edgan & Kadushin, 1995, Kadushin, 1996; McCullock & Brown, 1970; McNeil et al., 1998; Cowles. 2000; Rizzo & Abrams, 2000). It appears that, in today's practice environment, many individuals outside the discipline continue to remain unsure of what the health care social worker does, including in the emergency room. In addition, many times social workers themselves disagree over what constitutes "health care" social work (Dziegielewski, 1998). This is true despite the affirmation of health care social work as a discipline by the National Association of Social Workers (NASW, 1996).

According to the NASW' *(1996),* social work services shall be an integral part of every health care organization. The services shall be provided to individuals, their families and significant others; to special population groups; to communities; and to special health-related programs and educational systems **(NASW,** 1996).

In the opinion of this researcher and others (Abramson & Rosenthal, 1995; Benett, 1973; Cowles; 2000; Mizrahi & Abramson, 1985; Soskis, 1985) the role of the social worker in the emergency room is to provide clinical and concrete services, in assisting patients coping with crisis such as sudden death, domestic violence, child abuse, elderly abuse, homelessness, substance abuse and issues of discharge planning. Concrete services are those that revolve around resource information and referral activities. They include linking the patient with resources that can, for example, assist with arrangements for admission and aftercare, care of the patient's family during his/ her absence or disability, assistance with transportation, telephone calls, or helping to obtain medical aids and appliances. Clinical services are the various forms of counseling involving a process of interpersonal interaction between the social worker and the client. The focus here is on attitudes, feelings, perceptions, decisions or behaviors of the client.

Frequently, such services target client problems that are related to adjustment to the health service or facility or to the diagnosis, prognosis or medical treatment plan (Cowles, 2000).

It is crucial that social workers explain to medical staff, hospital administration and the public the importance of their clinical interventions and the value of their services (Wrenn & Rice, 1994; Cowles, 2000). This is especially true with the advent of managed care, which has challenged all health care professionals to show that what they do is necessary, effective, and cost-efficient. This means that the interventions that social workers provide must be socially acknowledged as necessary as well as therapeutically effective and cost-efficient. (Chethan & McVor, 1992; Cowless, 2000). In addition, these services must be professionally competitive with other disciplines (medicine, nursing, psychology and psychiatry) that claim similar treatment strategies and techniques (Dziegielewsk 1998). This is especially true for social workers in the emergency room where lack of understanding of their professional role may prevent doctors and nurses from referring patients experiencing medical emergencies for social work intervention.

By shifting from a fee-for-service system to a pre-paid service system, some financial incentive was provided to physicians and other health care providers to focus on "health maintenance" (Mizrahi, 1993). Today, however, managed care seems little involved in preventive care (Munson, 1997) and more involved in preventing health service providers from using interventions that are not established by outcomes research as cost-effective. In essence, the social worker in the emergency room becomes an agent of managed care and agrees to serve the public within the corporate guidelines and not necessarily according to the assessed needs of the patient.

According to Mizrahi & Abramson (2000), the impact of managed care on collaborative relationships is yet unclear, although health care providers, particularly physicians, have clearly experienced reduced autonomy in patient care decision-making. Furthermore, social workers in health care settings are faced with a need for clinical intervention in patient health care education, clinical practice dilemmas, greater consumer diversity, need for more social work research, and the need to reexamine what social workers do in health care (Browne et al., 1996).

Because hospital-based social work has not typically been income generating, social work departments have been vulnerable to downsizing and elimination (Rizzo & Abrams, 2000). Where social work services have been retained, most time is spent in negotiating with managed care companies and providing concrete services to patients, such as arranging transportation or telephone calls (Eggan & Kadushin, 1995).

One purpose of social work is to alleviate distress and achieve goals that are important to clients (Gibelman, 1995). Social work in health care refers both to *direct* practice, which is based on face- to-face interactions with the client and the family, and *indirect* practice, which involves interactions with representatives of clients, agencies, and communities (Gibelman, 1995). Social work's unique perspective, stated in its most simplistic form, is that of recognizing the importance of the "individual-in-situation" or the "person-in- environment" (Hepworth & Larsen, 1993; Skidmore, Thackeray, & Farley, 1997).

Social Work in the Emergency Room

Social work in the emergency room is a non-traditional specialty that involves working with physicians, and nurses who are typically more attuned to illness and trauma than to patients' social needs (Elliot, 1987). The role of the social worker in the emergency room is to collaborate with physicians, nurses, and other medical staff (Mizrahi & Abramson, 1985; Abramson & Rosenthal, 1995), to identify the social needs of patients, not just the presenting problem. The social worker contributes to the overall effectiveness of the operation of the emergency room by helping patients cope with their crises, including sudden death, domestic violence, child abuse, elderly abuse, homelessness, substance abuse, as well as with issues of discharge planning.

Using the construct provided by Soskis (1985) and Cowles (2000) in regards to social work functions in hospital settings, the roles of the social worker in the emergency room can be outlined as follows:

- an advocate for patient rights,
- a broker who knows all the relevant resources and can link the patient with the most appropriate ones.
- a consultant who provides expert opinions to others when asked,
- a counselor who engages in personalized interpersonal interaction with a patient probing the patient's feelings, attitudes or behaviors,
- a liaison who acts as a bridge between two or more people or organizations,
- a mediator who facilitates conflict resolution between parties;
- a planner who prepares a course of action, and
- a teacher who transmits knowledge to others.

A review of studies about social work practice in hospital settings from 1967 through 2000, provides little knowledge about social work programs in emergency rooms. There is no information on how many programs there are throughout the country; how many social workers are employed in them; what kind of training these workers have or the administrative structures and service pattern of these units.

The efficient use of social workers in the emergency room depends in large part on how the other professionals perceive social work practice. Those outside the social work profession may not be familiar with the range of services and skills provided by social workers. The health care delivery system may limit social work to provide only concrete services and fail to utilize the social worker's skills in helping patients cope with the emotional impact of illness and hospitalization. Lack of knowledge of what social workers do can create conflict in collaborating with other professionals in the provision of services.. The data in this study will contribute to understanding how social work is viewed in the emergency room so students working in this setting can plan realistic interventions acceptable to all emergency room staff.

The research questions that guide this study are:

1. What are the differences in perceptions among social workers, doctors and nurses regarding social workers' roles in the medical emergency room?
2. Is there a difference in role perceptions between municipal and voluntary hospitals?
3. How can social work education better address the need for the social worker's presence in the emergency room?

This study examined the following hypotheses:

1. Perceptions of social workers' roles in the medical emergency room will vary significantly by profession: Social Work, Medicine, and Nursing.

   a) Physicians and nurses are more likely to perceive social workers' roles as providing concrete rather than clinical services.
   b) Social workers perceive their roles as providing both, concrete and clinical services.

2. There will be no significant differences among doctors and nurses in their perceptions of social workers' roles in the emergency room by type of hospital (municipal and voluntary).

Sample Description

The sample included 38 social workers, 39 doctors, and 40 registered nurses in hospital emergency rooms in the New York City area. The hospitals that participated in the study were selected from the 1998-1999 edition of the American Hospital Association Guide (1961). A list of 24 municipal and voluntary hospitals was compiled from this source. Administrators at 20 of the 24 hospitals contacted agreed, verbally and in writing, to support their staff's participation in the study. Four did not respond. The hospitals in the study range in size from 425 to 890 beds.

Literature Review

Several studies about health care professional and expectations of social work in hospital settings from 1967 through 2000 were reviewed (Olsen & Olsen, 1967; McCulloch & Brown, 1970; Phillips. McCulloch & Brown, and Hambro, 1971; Carrigan, 1974; Cowles & Lefcowitz, 1992; Koeske, Koeske, & Mallinger, 1993; Egan & Kadushin, 1995; Kadushin, 1996; Auslander & Schneidman, 1996; McNeil, Nicholas, Szechy & Lach, 1998; Cowles. 2000). These studies show that social workers define their functions broadly, focusing on the whole person and including the patient, hospital. and community in professional decisions. In other studies, doctors, nurses, and patients alike have been found to have more narrow views of social workers as "gofers" (Cowles & Lefcowitz, 1992).

Limitations of the Study

This study is limited to perceptions of social workers, doctors, and nurses about the roles of social workers in medical emergency rooms in New York City. A second limitation is that the respondents were self-selected in responding to the survey. There is no data on the number of potential participants in the hospitals surveyed. Further, the actual roles of social workers in the various emergency rooms are not known. There may also be differences in the instrument's validity and reliability from what Carrigan (1974) reported due to changes made for this study from the original instrument. Other limitations include that it is a study of perceptions rather than efficacy; that it was conducted on a one-time basis, with one group-study design; and its inability to generalize from one geographical location to the larger population.

Anticipated Contributions

The study will provide information on how social workers are perceived by professionals in other disciplines in the emergency room, namely doctors and nurses. It will also tell us how social workers perceive their own roles. This study will also provide information on whether perceptions of social work roles vary according to the type of hospital, public or voluntary, where social workers are employed in emergency rooms.

The findings will contrast and compare the views of other medical professionals with the views of social workers about their own roles in the emergency room.

This research will contribute to social policy as it reinforces the need to inform and educate health care professionals and administrators about the range of skills and roles that should be performed by social workers in the emergency room. In addition, this research can be used to indicate the extent to which social workers are being fully utilized in emergency rooms. As managed care becomes increasingly a dominant mode of health care delivery, it will be increasingly important for health care administrators to fully utilize the skills of the professional staff (Cowles, 2000). The data from this study can be used to better advocate for social workers in emergency room settings and to help those in these settings understand the obstacles they face in working with their colleagues.

Davidson (1998), citing Monkman (1991) and Ell (1996), wrote: "The benefits to patients need to be the primary concerns of social workers in all settings, including the emergency room." It remains imperative for social workers to demonstrate, through research studies, that the professional expertise that allows them to provide *supportive services* to clients provides positive and welcome results for clients, such as reduction of lost work or school days; decreased stress-induced illness; and fewer of the medical crises that are often related to lack of knowledge, non-compliance with treatment, and overburdened caretaker (Davidson, 1998). Research can be used to advocate for provision of psychosocial services throughout health care programs (Davidson, 1998).

For years, literature in the field of social work in health care has called for social workers to "demonstrate their effectiveness" if they hope to retain their positions in the field. This call for outcomes research has not been sufficiently heeded. Now there is growing evidence that social work is not widely recognized as a key health care profession (Rosenberg, 1998).

Rosenberg (1998) points to the following factors as barriers to social work being accorded a firm position in the health field: its association with a relatively powerless-welfare" clientele; its perception as competition for physicians; its failure to demonstrate the cost-effectiveness of its services; its being seen as ineffective in resolving social problems (which require the cooperation of powers beyond social work alone); its lack of outcome data to develop "best practices," as well as its failure to employ quality management processes; its lack of effective collaboration with other health care professionals to address social health problems; and its lack of a "track record" of work to improve public social health policy.

Currently in the emergency room setting a social worker usually provides patient discharge planning, such as organizing transportation, and providing options for post discharge patient management. Social workers are perceived by doctors and nurses as a small group of individuals that provide concrete services such as determining eligibility of patients for social services, acting as liaison between doctors and patients, and reporting patients' feelings to physicians. Doctors and nurses most frequently refer patients for social work intervention when these types of concrete services are needed (Cowles, 2000). Social workers are also perceived as patient helpers at several levels including. but not limited to, obtaining medical appliances, strengthening patients' participation in their own care, and conducting pre-discharge study of home environments.

The perception of the social worker is one of an employee subordinate to doctors and nurses. This narrow perception needs to be expanded to include the range of roles that the social worker can potentially perform in the emergency room. These roles encompass the provision of concrete services included above and other duties such as assessment of patients' psychosocial needs, referring patients for psychiatric evaluation and presenting to the community the social work services available in the emergency room.

The findings in this study show that more education and training about the role of the social worker in the hospital emergency room is also needed for social workers.

Education would emphasize not only the content of social work in the emergency room but also training in the skills needed to demonstrate and communicate this to the medical and nursing staff. Social work students preparing for hospital social work need to be taught how to set limits in carrying out institutional policies to avoid compromising professional autonomy and responsibility (Kadushin & Kulys, 1995).

Most of the descriptive literature about social work in emergency rooms emphasizes the necessity of relieving the rest of the staff from dealing with social/emotional problems, rather than the medical/ surgical problems that are their primary concerns. The social worker is the professional uniquely trained to perform this role and thus contribute to the provision of quality patient care. This study provides a better understanding of the need for stronger support for social workers in this setting and, through this, helps emergency room staff more fully serve the needs of the community.

CHAPTER TWO

The Study Problem

The Effect of Managed Care on Hospitals and the Provision of Social Work Services

Hospital social workers have lost ground through deregulation and closing of Social Work Departments as managed care has transformed hospitals from revenue generating components of health care delivery systems to lower cost outpatient venues (Cowles, 2000). The development of Medicaid and Medicare programs has affected social work practice in hospital settings, largely as a result of government efforts to control the cost of health care (Cowles, 2000). One effect of these cost-control efforts has been a general trend toward limiting social work services reimbursable by the two main government health insurance programs to those that are related to the patient's current health condition. The fear of not being reimbursed has led to a general tendency to limit services to those, which are essential. Since the two government financing programs only reimburse services that are ordered or approved by the physician, this too has acted as a constrain on the provision of social work services (Cowles, 2000).

According to Cummings & Abell (1993), the need for radical change in the health care field is gaining support. Hospitals are feeling the pressure of hard economic times as decreasing reimbursements, changing service delivery patterns, and increased competition are forcing them to reduce cost while maintaining quality.

The federal government efforts to contain the rapid increase in health care costs led to passage of the Tax Equity and Fiscal Responsibility Act in 1993, which established the familiar DRG (diagnosis-related group) system. This system limits the length of stay of hospitalized patients to a prescribed period of time, depending on the diagnosis.

Overstays must be paid by the hospital itself. not the patient. Thus, the overall effect of the DRG system has been earlier release of most patients. This reduction in length of stay has further constrained what social workers can attempt to do with inpatients and places even greater priority on the social worker's function of assisting with arrangements for post-hospital continuity of care in a nursing home, home care, or other plan (Cowles, 2000).

The expansion of managed care could have two possible consequences for social work in the emergency room. On the one hand, it could lead to a more rational use of social work services, so that medical and nursing staff is more focused on providing health care, and social workers are designated to address psychosocial issues. On the other hand, in an effort to reduce the most of health care staff, social work departments could be stripped from social workers altogether, and when such needs arise, they could be provided haphazardly or not at all by an overworked medical staff or by other unqualified personnel.

Defining Managed Care

Managed care is a term that describes "the range of alternative financial vehicles to traditional indemnity health insurance leading to greater elements of control and accountability in health cost and quality." Managed care is built on a financial incentive to limit services (Kotelchuck, 1994; Austin, 1995). For example, inpatient days, traditionally a major contributor to hospital revenue streams, have declined. Through closing inpatient units by contracting with one provider organization to provide health care services across the whole continuum of care, from primary to tertiary, millions of dollars can be saved on facilities, operations, and staffing (Austin, 1995).

The profit motive causes inherent systematic strains on hospitals struggling to serve the poor under managed care. Many managed care organizations are accustomed to serving employed, low-risk populations and have little experience providing support services such as outreach, case management, transportation, and other psychosocial services that are beneficial to high risk populations. Patients requiring extensive psychosocial and support services encounter difficulty in obtaining a full range of health and related social services that they need under these plans (Douglas & Torres, 1994).

Medical centers have experienced a drastic reduction in both private and public sector reimbursements for care delivered to patients. In the private sector, managed care has led to a decrease in the number of patients who are admitted to hospitals, in the number of patients days, and has reduced the overall of reimbursement for all care given (Baxt, 2000). In the public sector, as a result of the Welfare Act of 1996 and other state driven legislation, states have reduced eligibility for welfare (Baxt, 2000). Welfare reforms have further increased the number of uninsured in America. As Americans move from welfare to full-time, but low-paying, jobs, they lose their Medicaid insurance, only to find not only that many small business do not provide health insurance but also that they cannot afford health care insurance (Carrasquillo; Himmelstein; Woolhandler; Bor, 1999). New York State announced that it had 500 million of unspent Medicaid funds.

The net result has been the increase in the indigent uninsured (Kuttner, 1999). Forty three million Americans were uninsured and thirty three million were underinsured for the entire year in 1999 (Grumbach, 2000). The US Census Bureau indicates that approximately 8% of households with an annual income of $75,000 or more have no health insurance (Krauss, 1998). For the uninsured, access to health care services is a growing problem, partly exacerbated by the rise of managed care. Now, poor people do not have the option of seeing a private physician in the community. Instead they depend on the emergency room for their entire medical needs (Sherer, 1999).

As pointed out by Dalen (2000), during the 1990s, the number of Americans with optimum health care has diminished such that they have become an "endangered species." The payers of health care, employers and the government, found the cost of providing health care to be unacceptably high. Health care costs Skyrocketed in the 1980s and early 1990s. By 1998, health care costs in the United States were $1.2 trillion, 15% of the gross national product-the highest in the world (Dalen, 2000; & Ginzberg, 1999).

For the low-income patient, issues of exclusion are always a concern because they are "too poor" to afford insurance but are "too rich" to qualify for Medicaid benefits.

They make too much money to qualify for Medicaid but too little money to afford health insurance (Dalen, 2000). Although Medicaid offers a range of health care services to the poor, many patients continue to fall between the cracks of the complex bureaucracy of the health care delivery system. The majority of Medicaid recipients are women with children or families with very low incomes. Single adults, however, are often not eligible for Medicaid because many states regard them as able bodied capable of gainful employment. The Kaiser Commission on Medicaid and the Uninsured reported in August 1999 that "because men are less likely to be single parents, they are also less likely to qualified for Medicaid coverage and therefore more likely to be uninsured than women with low incomes. Over half (53%) of poor men are uninsured (Atkatz, 1994; Sherer, 1999).

A high proportion of homeless adults and household low income with no dependents are both medically indigent and untouched by private health insurance (Douglasfforres, 1994; Sidel, 1990; National Center for Health Statistics, 2000). Localities have dealt with this issue in a variety of ways. When indigent patients seek health care in hospitals' emergency rooms or clinics, the institution typically absorbs the cost of care or directly bills the local government. However, local governments are increasingly unable or unwilling to absorb costs; *hospitals are increasingly encouraged to triage patients back to hospitals in the patient's area of residence to avoid the probability of non-payment of incurred expenses.*

Consequences of Managed Care in Emergency Rooms

In hospital emergency departments, the tension between the goal of cost containment and quality of care is in direct conflict (Aghabian & McQuaide, 1992; Clement & Klingbeil, 1981; Markovchich & Wolfe, 1993). Under federal law, a hospital must provide an appropriate medical examination to any person who requests care in its emergency room. Hospitals must also provide any treatment needed to stabilize a patient's condition (National Center for Health Statistics. 1994; Knopp, Biros, White, Waeckerle, 2000). Uninsured patients have little choice but to get even the most routine care in emergency rooms, which by law must treat every patient who shows up. In New York. the Commonwealth Fund found that the greatest number of people using the emergency room for primary care tended not to be those with the worst insurance, but those who lived in the poorest neighborhoods, where there were few doctors and more language and cultural barriers (Knopp, Biros, White, Weckerle, 2000).

Hospitals report that HMOs are increasingly denying claims for care provided in their emergency rooms. This problem sets up a reactive pattern on the part of patients who are reluctant to seek emergency services early on. Physicians too, have to weigh how much care to provide based on whether the hospital will be paid. In addition, the threat of malpractice litigation has prompted what Side! (1990) referred as "defensive medicine" as emergency room doctors order expensive tests to rule out various medical concerns in order to protect themselves from lawsuits.

Problems of quality of care have focused on the obvious intrusion of managed care on the doctor-patient relationship. Practicing physicians have adapted to managed care by reducing office visits, specialty referrals, and inpatient days. Physicians in emergency rooms have been pressured to see more patients per hour, a practice that can lead to poor clinical results and low patient satisfaction (Side!, 1990; Iglehart, 1992; National Center for Health Statistics, 2000).

Berger, Cayner, Jenses, Mizrahi. Sceny & Tachtenberg (1996), collaborated in a national study of the changes affecting social work services in a sample of 340 hospitals for the fiscal year of 1992 to

1994. Their findings suggest that the changes affecting social work need to be viewed within the context of the dramatic changes occurring in the hospital and health care field. About one-third of the social work departments reported changes in the social work director, and an equal number of respondents indicated that departmental functions had been reviewed. These two factors could combine to create a feeling of departmental instability and vulnerability. Threats to the department may take on greater significance in the absence of stable leadership. Even a small reduction could be interpreted as impending doom if staff does not perceive that their leadership is capable of providing direction and protection during such chaotic times (Berger, 1996).

Quality of care has also been compromised in hospitals through the deregulation and closing social work departments as a mechanism of cost cutting. Because hospital based social work typically has not been income generating, social work departments have been vulnerable to downsizing and elimination (Rizzo & Abrams, 2000). Where social work services have been retained, most of the workers' time is spent in negotiating with managed care companies and providing concrete services to patients, such as arranging for transportation or telephone calls (Eggan & Kadushin, 1995).

The Practice Problem

The role of the social worker in the emergency room

Historically the role of the social worker in the emergency room included the assessment of patients whose varied individual and psychosocial problems are at the same time public issues (Bergman, 1976; Healey, 1981; Soskis, 1985; Heggar, 1993). When patients arrive to the emergency room, they are often sicker than they were in the past; and when they are discharged from the hospital, they are barely well. Homeless patients are referred to shelters, drug addicts and alcoholics to drug and alcohol programs, patients with psychiatric problems are referred for psychiatric evaluation, referral for Medicaid benefits are made for those patients who lack medical insurance and are in need of medical care (Soskis, 1985; Heggar, 1993).

The role of social workers in the emergency room is also collaborative, since they share the same goal as the medical staff, which is to help in providing health care services to all who come to the emergency room in need of treatment despite their income or resources (Abramson & Mizrahi, 1987). According to Abramson and Mizrahi (1996); Mailick (1981); Rehr; Blumenfield; & Rosenberg (1998), the rationale for social work participation in collaborative activities is based on the recognition of the complexity of human problems, the high degree of knowledge, technology, and skills needed to meet them, the specialization of function, and the resulting requirements of coordination and integration of the work of providers on behalf of patients. The nature of the crisis that leads to the emergency room presents many opportunities for collaboration between medicine and social work. Such collaborations can lead to increased efficiency in the emergency room. This partnership can prevent patients from getting lost in the complex health care system.

There are many ways in which social workers provide assistance to physicians in relation to direct patient care (Abramson & Mizrahi, 1996). Social workers enhance physicians' effectiveness with patients by sharing knowledge about the cultural and environmental background of a particular patient.

The effectiveness of the emergency room depends on the ability of the system to provide adequate solutions to the problems faced by the hospital as a whole. Hospitals functioning under the Diagnostic Related Group (DRG) prospective payment reimbursement system must be concerned with effecting timely discharges for their patients.

The placement of social workers in the emergency room was made more urgent with the introduction of the DRG early intervention approach, which emphasized to avoid unnecessary admissions and to mobilize patients from the emergency room (Soskis, 1985).

With the onset of managed care, however, the traditional procedures for providing social work and health care services have completely changed (Cowles, 2000). A new vocabulary now applies as evidenced in such terms as "exclusive provider organizations," "medical necessity," and "capitation." A careful review of the profession's history and core concepts, however, demonstrates that many of the principles and techniques of social work are compatible in regard to mandates for high quality, functionally oriented, cost-effective care (Soskis, 1985; Cowles, 2000). This compatibility is predicated among other medical professionals about how to effectively maximize social workers' skills in moving patients through the service system of the hospital emergency room.

The Evolution of Emergency Medicine

To comprehend the full impact of the revolutionary change in emergency medicine, it is necessary to have traced the events that led to today's emergency medicine system. Emergency medicine developed because of the population and the breakdown of the traditional orientation of the family physician. When people became sick after finding themselves in unfamiliar places they often sought and expected medical attention. Industries began to operate 24 hours a day, and the orientation of the population in expecting medical services to be available around the clock, stimulated the development of emergency facilities (Schwarts; Safar; & Wagner, 1986). The convenience and the feeling of security and protection and availability that such facilities emanated answered the public's need.

According to Schwarts; Safar; & Wagner (1986), three important elements are considered as major stimulants for the development of emergency medicine:

1. Patients' need and demand for emergency medical services.
2. Changes modes of medical practice.
3. Expansion of technological developments and the consequent opportunities for rapid diagnosis.

Each of these factors has exerted complementary stimulation from different directions, i.e., from the patient, hospital medical community, and physicians (Schwarts; Safar; & Wagner, 1986). The first of these determinants, the needs and demands of patients, reflects changes that have occurred in American society, particularly in the last five decades. The art and science of medicine involve intimate and extensive work with people; the needs of society have modified and shaped the development of medical techniques and practice.

The second major stimulating factor is the changing role of the modem hospital and simultaneous changes in modes of medical practice. The hospital's increase in social and community concerns, responding both to patients' demands and self-interest, led to the creation of emergency rooms in 1954. Hospitals recognized that by having a viable emergency department fills beds and makes use of existing services more extensively; a hospital in a marginal financial situation could move into the black through revenues derived from their emergency unit. Hospitals in heavily populated areas require 24-hour coverage in the emergency room (Schwarts; Safar; & Wagner, 1986).

In 1975, the American Medical Association's House of Delegates recommended to their Council on Medical education (CME) that emergency medicine be defined as a new specialty for accreditation and certification, comparable to other specialty areas (Schwarts; Safar; & Wagner, 1986). In 1979, emergency medicine was recognized as a specialty (Duncan & MacMahon, 1981). The first specialty boards were given in 1980, for the first time, there was a group of physicians trained specifically in emergency medicine and tested as to their competence (Soskis, 1985; Schwarts; Safar; & Wagner, 1986). Emergency medicine is the thirtieth largest specialty (Schwarts; Safar; & Wagner, 1986). Originally, emergency rooms were set as the first place where patients had to go before being admitted to the hospital. Later, they were referred to as accident dispensaries, since the emergency rooms were designed to treat acute trauma for those who survived long enough to get there (Soskis, 1985). Presently, emergency rooms serve as the providers of services for patients with multiple medical social, and psychological problems (National Center for Health statistics, 2000; Knobb, Biros, Waeckerle, 2000)

The modem emergency room performs a service that is oriented to the consumer. The mission of the emergency room is to treat everyone with as much humanity as can be mustered, with special skill for the most acutely ill or injured patients. As a major clinical department, it interacts with all the other departments in a constant working relationship to provide high-quality medical care (Clement & Klingbeil, 1981; Prescott, 1998). As the need for a more organized and effective emergency room service became evident, in 1981. the Joint Commission on the Accreditation of Hospital Organizations (JCAHO) made appropriate findings and recommendations for the establishment of this department within the hospitals.

Major developments contributing to the increased use of the emergency room, according to Soskis (1985); Mizrahi (1995) include the following:

- The medical advances developed in the two World Wars and the Korean war, led to great improvement in trauma care, so that people can now reach the emergency room alive.
- The concentration of resources in hospitals and their availability 24-hours has become standard services, especially when physicians have restricted hours and outside visits.
- Many insurance companies cover visits to the emergency room, but not to doctor's office.
- Inner city neighborhoods lack physicians, but not hospitals.
- Cutbacks were made in social service programs providing free health care clinics, psychiatric outpatient care and other services.
- The deinstitutionalization of psychiatric patients, many of whom are unable to maintain themselves, increased emergency service demands.

In 1954, the nation's hospitals reported 17 patient-visits to the emergency room; in 1958, there were 18 million visits; in 1968, there were 44 million visits; and in 1977, it rose to 76 million visits (O'Boyle, Davis, & Kraf, 1985: Schwatrs, 1986). Most of the 100 million Americans who visit the emergency rooms each year do not need immediate medical attention (National Center for Health statistics, 2000). One aspect for the increase use of the emergency rooms is that emergency rooms are the one entry point and treatment site in the health care arena that can neither deny nor delay access (Schwarts; Safar; & Wagner. 1986; Mizrahi, 1995; JCAHO, 1998).

Impact of Mandated Emergency Care

At one time, the Common Law did not require a physician or hospital to provide medical treatment to all that sought it. Thus, private hospitals, voluntary hospitals could refuse to treat patients needing emergency care. A series of abuses of the privilege not to provide emergency care and legal decisions have almost completely reversed this doctrine. As a result, hospitals may have no right to refuse to treat people who seek medical treatment in the emergency room (Schwarts; Safar; & Wagner, 1986).

Federal legislation, such as the Hill-Burton Act (Mizrahi, 1995), has significantly restricted a hospital's right to refuse emergency medical care. A hospital that has received a Hill-Burton grant from the federal government has the responsibility to provide a certain amount of "free" medical care to indigent patients.

State laws and regulations have also mandated that hospitals have the duty to provide emergency medical care. Accrediting organizations such as the Joint Commission on accreditation of Hospital Organizations (JCAHO, 1998) have also affirmed the duty to provide emergency medical care. For example, New York has adopted the following law: "In cities with a population of one million or more, a general hospital must provide emergency medical treatment to all persons in need of such care and treatment" (Schwarts, et al., 1986; Rosen; Baker; Braden; Dailey; & Levy, 1998; JCAHO, 1998). Accrediting organizations, such as the Joint Commission on Accreditation of Hospital Organizations (JCAHO, 1998), have affirmed the duty to provide emergency medical care. Based on these laws and regulations, hospitals and emergency room practitioners have a duty to provide treatment to all persons in need.

Social Workers in the Emergency Room in the Era of Managed Care

The emergency room is a major entryway into the health care system for a substantial number of people (Bergman, 1976; Schwarts; Safar; & Wagner, 1986). The major users of emergency rooms for non-acute medical problems are poor rather than rich, poorly educated rather than well-educated, urban rather than rural, people of low social status and high family mobility, people with no medical coverage and lacking relationships with private physicians. Trauma is no longer the main business of the emergency department (Soskis, 1985; Knobb, Biros, White, Waeckerle, 2000).

According to Knobb, Biros, White, Waeckerle (2000), the use of the emergency room for nonurgent care is growing. Emergency room visits are increasing every year for about 20 percent from 1985 to 2000. Out of total users, the emergency room physicians saw about 85 percent more patients with nonurgent problems during the same period.

Emergency rooms, especially in urban areas such as the South Bronx, are becoming overburdened which vastly compound the difficulties of providing effective medical care to the emergency victim.

Benett (1973) reports that social workers were introduced into the Emergency Department of Brooklyn Hospital in 1972 to help with difficult social/or psychologically disturbed patients.

Persons outside the social work profession may not be familiar with the range of services and skills offered by social workers. The system may limit social work services to only concrete services and fail to utilize the social workers' skills to help patients with the emotional impact of illness and hospitalization. Lack of knowledge of what social workers do also creates conflict in collaboration with other professionals in the provision of services. The efficient use of social workers in the emergency room depends in large part on how other professionals perceive social work practice.

CHAPTER THREE

Literature Review

Several studies about health care professional and expectations of social work in hospital settings from 1967 through 2000 were reviewed. These studies show that social workers define their functions broadly, focusing on the whole person and including the patient, hospital, and community in professional decisions. Doctors, nurses, and patients alike have been found to have more narrow views of social workers as "'gofers" (Cowles & Lefcowitz, 1992).

Physicians Perception of Medical Social Workers' Role

An early study by Olsen and Olsen (1967) investigated actual and perceived expectations among both physicians and social workers concerning the role of the social worker in a medical setting. Their study explored two facets of this issue: (1) physicians' and social workers' expectations of the appropriate scope and content of the role of the social worker in a hospital; and (2) physicians' and social workers' views of how the other group perceives the social workers' role. The general proposition underlying this research was that considerable conflict existed between physicians and social workers in expectations and perceptions of the role of the social worker in the medical setting. The authors analyzed the role conflict that existed between physicians and social workers and the extent to which each professional group anticipated experiencing their role conflict.

The data were gathered by means of a self-administered questionnaire, given to all social workers and a random sample of physicians working at the university of Michigan Medical Center concerning role expectations and 15 types of activities for which medical social workers sometimes take responsibility (Olsen & Olsen, 1967). The researchers found a considerable amount of conflict between physicians and social workers, both in expectations and perceptions of the social workers' role. Physicians in this study were willing to grant fewer professional responsibilities to social workers than these social workers thought they should have. In 9 of the 15 activity areas investigated, they were less likely than social workers to include specific responsibilities within the social worker's professional role. Physicians were found to be more conservative in delegating responsibilities to social workers in regard to screening patients for psychiatric evaluation, helping patients with social and emotional problems related to medical situation, helping patients to adjust to the hospital, and deciding when patients' social and emotional problems are severe enough to affect their recovery. Physicians thought that arranging for post-hospital care was the social worker's only responsibility. Both physicians and social workers agreed that social workers expect to coordinate professional services, decide on post-hospital care and make referrals to community services.

McCulloch and Brown (1970) studied the responses of a randomly selected group of physicians in Birmingham, England, who were asked to rank order a list of functions that would be allocated to social workers if they were made readily available to the physicians' practices. The physicians agreed that they would use social workers primarily for concrete services, such as escorting patients to their institutions or agencies, or dealing with financial problems. It was found that physicians tended to see social workers more as environmental manipulators than professionals who deal with the psychosocial problems of patients and families.

The findings of Phillips et al. (1971), in their study of Boston's Israel Hospital, paralleled those of the British study in indicating a preponderance of requests for social work intervention on behalf of patients age 65 and over. Emphasis was placed on the provision of concrete services, such as dealing with financial problems, with the implicit expectation that the social worker would deal with the patient in need of concrete services, but with little appreciation that the worker's area of competence is working with the patient. Social workers' skills lie in working with psychosocial problems within family structures. Although physicians in the abstract may understand this role, they had not accepted it in practice. Physicians expect social workers to perform instrumental tasks such as providing assistance for language translation and locating nursing homes, arranging for post-hospital care, and making referrals to community resources.

Other Professionals' Perceptions of the Roles of Social Workers in Hospital Settings

Carrigan (1974) investigated the factors that influenced the definition of interdisciplinary social work practice in health care settings. She also examined factors that might affect professional perceptions of the social work role, such as the degree of professional contact with social workers or professional orientation to social work. Her study was conducted in two Veterans' Administration hospitals associated with medical and social work schools. The sample included 181 staff psychiatrists, psychologists, registered nurses, social workers, and administrators who were surveyed on their perceptions about the activities that social workers actually perform. The areas studied were:

- Technical mediation (e.g., professional consultations, informing medical staff of socioemotional-emotional functioning of patients);
- Reporting of patients, medical symptoms;
- Counseling (e.g., psychosocial assessments, provision of counseling and therapy to patients);
- Community mediation (e.g., agency referrals, arranging for extended care, placement in aftercare facilities); and

- Administration (e.g., coordination of services to patients, convening professional conferences, consultation on social welfare needs of patients, orienting medical and nursing staff to social work functions).

Social workers and other professional groups (psychiatrists, psychologists, and registered nurses) agreed with social workers on the extent to which social workers were performing indirect professional services (Carrigan, 1974). However, other professional groups perceived social workers as performing more community mediation and technical mediation. This was also true in the areas of technical mediation. On all other sub-scales, social worker's expectations of their own activities was more broad than the expectations of other professionals.

Carrigan (1974) concluded that the medical and nursing staff did not expect the social workers to perform more highly skilled functions such as counseling or administrative services.

Cowles and Lefcowitz (1992) studied of inter-professional role expectations of medical social workers and sought to facilitate a resolution of any differences between them. They found that social workers in hospitals think that other health care professionals, especially physicians, misunderstand their role in direct services. Other professional groups and the general public are inclined to perceive the social work function to be distinguished by a narrower focus than social workers on social environmental problems of people and on linking them with community resources and external support of their family.

In this study, self-administered questionnaires were distributed to a random sample of physicians (n=658), registered nurses (n=603) and all medical social workers (n=48) in these hospitals. Participants were asked to indicate whose job it was to perform 25 tasks included in four sets of seven generic tasks. Each set varied by the problems addressed (social-environmental or emotional), by the client (patient or family), and by the activity (assess, treat or refer). The tasks directed to the socio-environmental problems of patients were as follows:

- Assess the social-environmental problems of the patient.
- Help patients examine possible solutions to their social-environmental problems.
- Help patients of community resources for their social-environmental problems.
- Inform patients of community resources for their social-environmental problems of patients.
- Contact community agencies to request services for the social-environmental problems of patients.
- Assist patients in completing any application forms or procedures to obtain the community resources they need for their social-environmental problems.
- Inform patients of how their physical health condition may create social-environmental problems for them.
- Refer patients to appropriate hospital personnel for assistance with their social environmental problems.

The social work respondents believed that tasks dealing with social environmental problems of patients were clearly within the social work domain. Seventy percent of respondents believed that assisting patients in completing applications for needed community resources were the job of the social worker. Physicians and nurses expected the distinctive role of the social worker to be limited to referrals (instrumental linkage activity to assist patients and families in obtaining the community resources they needed for their social-environmental and emotional problems). The only task that the majority of physicians and nurses thought was outside the domain of social work was the assessment of the emotional problems of patients.

Perceptions of Mental Health Professionals of Social work in Hospital Settings

Koeske, Koeske, and Mallinger (1993) examined the perceptions of professional competence among psychologists, social workers, psychiatrists, and nurses in psychiatric hospital. Their study was designed to examine perception of self versus others, using multiple measures of evaluative perception. The research question was, "how do mental health professionals perceive one another?" The sample included 101 professionals engaged in clinical and counseling work. The findings in their study showed that there was a tendency for psychologists to rate social workers least favorably in terms of their competence as mental health care workers. Nurses rated psychiatrists as significantly more competent than social workers, the psychologists rated themselves as more competent than social workers and psychiatrists, and psychiatrists, rated social workers as less competent than other professionals. Nurses and social workers did not perceive differences in their own expertise relative to each other. Social workers were perceived as exhibiting greater warmth than psychiatrists and psychologists, and psychiatrists and psychologists were perceived as having greater expertise.

Egan and Kadushin (1995) examined rural hospital nurses and social workers' perceptions of the domain of the social worker. Social workers and nurses were asked whether the nurse or the social worker was best qualified to perform generic hospital social service tasks:

- Helping the patient to adjust to hospital routine.
- Helping the patient to adjust to separation from family.
- Assessing the psychosocial functioning of the patient.
- Helping a family plan for discharge.
- Arranging for home equipment for the patient. Helping the patient cope with illness.
- Assessing the impact of illness on the patient's family.
- Counseling a family of a mentally ill member.
- Arranging for placement in a nursing home after discharge.
- Counseling a terminally ill patient.
- Assessing a patient's needs for psychiatric services.
- Helping families understand financial aspects of hospitalization.
- Assessing the patient's need for home health services.
- Helping a family to understand insurance/cost/aftercare.
- Evaluating a family's need for counseling.

Social workers perceived themselves to be better qualified than nurses in psychosocial assessments and in specific discharge planning (Egan & Kadushin. 1995). The nurses regarded social workers a-; best qualified to provide concrete services in the discharge planning process. Social workers and nurses disagreed most strongly on three tasks related to the assessment of the emotional functioning of the patient's family and on one counseling task related to the patient. Social workers and nurses agreed that social workers were better qualified than nurses to provide discharge planning.

Perceptions of Patients Regarding Social Workers' Roles

In another study, Kadushin (1996) interviewed elderly hospitalized patients and their social workers about their perceptions of the discharge planning process in two not for-profit acute care hospitals and one government sponsored hospital in West Virginia. Patients were interviewed approximately one day prior to discharge. The social workers were interviewed within hours of their patient's discharge. Questions were developed to elicit respondents' perceptions of the following aspects of the discharge planning process:

- The problems identified by both worker and patient.
- The problems of the social workers and patients about interventions implemented during the contact to address identified problems.
- Perceptions of the social workers and patients' understanding of the social work role at termination of contact.

Findings indicated that patients had vague expectations of the interaction with the social worker at the initiation of contact and generally developed their understanding of the social work role during discharge planning.

According to Kadushin (1996), the social worker's role unlike the role of the physician and nurse is not visible. Patients can understand doctoring and nursing by experiencing physical acts of care giving. Most of the social work role, however, occurs "behind the scenes," outside of the patient's experience, negotiating and consulting with other service providers. The behind-the-scenes quality of medical social work tends to make the social worker invisible to patients and often to other professional staff.

Auslander and Schneidman (1996) interviewed 120 discharged hospital social work patients about their assessment of social work services received in the acute care hospital setting. They were asked to define their psychosocial problems, list their expectations of the social work department, and appraise the outcome of the social work intervention. The study was conducted in two hospitals of the Hadassah Medical Organization-Hebrew University of Jerusalem. Patients were seen by a social worker at least once during a four- mouth period beyond the intake interview. The findings in this study showed that no clients expected social workers to be able to resolve their health problems. Twenty five percent of the clients stated that they had no expectations whatsoever from the social worker. Over one-fourth of the persons who cited a specific problem did not expect to get any help from the social worker.

McNeil et al. (1998) interviewed 83 parents of children at The Hospital for Sick Children, Toronto. Ontario. Canada, in which social work staff utilized a client centered approach and provide a range of services including counseling related to adjustment to illness and disability, liaison with community agencies, advocacy, and assistance with instrumental concerns.

Selected patients had received a wide spectrum of social work services ranging from one or two social work contacts to a prolonged period of intervention. Types of service also varied from practical and instrumental services (e.g. finding a community resource) to intense case centered therapies. The findings in this study showed that a large majority (87%) of respondents rated the service they received as either good or outstanding. Similarly (83.7%) reported some or a lot of improvement in their problems that led them to see a social worker. Overall analysis of the findings indicates that respondents valued the psychosocial services provided by the social worker. These findings support the importance of a social work service in pediatric hospitals that provides a holistic assessment of the patient/family and a client centered range of interventions.

Summary

The results of these studies are mixed. Some show that other health care professionals in hospital settings as well as patients have low expectations and misperceptions about social work role. Others show that the social work role is viewed in a more positive manner. The negative findings may be due to organizational factors affecting the delivery of social work services. The findings in these studies indicate that this is still a critical issue. The literature demonstrates that other professionals, especially medical doctors perceive that social workers are qualified primarily to engage in community liaison services and technical services such as securing medical equipment and treatment. These studies cited indicated that other health care professionals generally do not view social workers as competent to provide diagnosis of emotional or psychological problems or to treat them. They also do not view social workers' administrative activities as legitimate.

- According to Cowles (2000), depending on the characteristics of the organizational setting of practice, there may be constrains on social work intervention in terms of the following:
- Available time to work with clients when they are discharge.
- Which kinds of services are acceptable to organizational policy (for example, Catholic organizations are unlikely to allow social work interventions that facilitate access to abortion or "artificial" methods of contraception).
- Which staff members of the organization are allocated responsibility for which types of services.

For example, in some health settings, persons other than social workers may be assigned responsibility for pre-admission and or discharge planning or counseling. In addition, oftentimes, an interdisciplinary team of health care professionals, rather than an individual, jointly decides upon appropriate interventions (Cowles, 2000).

As pointed by Auslander (2000), it is very rare indeed for a patient to go to the emergency room for care because he/she needs assistance of a social worker. But it is quite possible that the medical problem, which brought that person to the hospital may cause psychosocial problems as well; and the care provided for that medical problem may actually lead to problems in other areas-psychosocial problems. To best provide this boundary-spanning service, hospital social work departments were developed.

For years we have taken as a forgone conclusion the notion that social work functions are best performed by a social work department within the hospital (Auslander, 2000). But in more than a few places around the world, this logic is being questioned.

So that not too long ago, in Great Britain, the organizational responsibility for social work in hospitals was moved out of hospitals and into the local authorities, that is the social welfare system (Rachman, 1997). Because hospital-based social work typically has not been income generating, social work departments have been vulnerable to downsizing and eliminated. In numerous hospitals around the world, social work departments, as discreet organizational entities, are being downsized or eliminated and the social workers dispersed throughout the institution (Rizzo & Abrams, 2000). And in Australia, social work departments in some states are having to show that the services they offer cannot be provided better and more economically by other organizations in a process known as "competitive neutrality" (NAHCC, 1997). Social workers are being challenged to demonstrate how their services contribute to the mission of the organization.

Since the 1970s, managed care organizations have tended to shift from predominately nonprofit to predominantly for-profit organizations with stockholder ownership. Furthermore, the theory behind the original health maintenance organization was that by focusing on primary and preventive care, health care costs could be controlled by reducing the need for more costly repair services from specialists (Cowles, 2000). By shifting from a fee for-service system to a prepaid service system, a mechanism of financial incentive was provided to physicians and other providers to focus on "health main-tenance" (Mizrahi, 1993; Cowles, 2000).

Today, however, managed care seems little involved in "preven-tive care" and more involved in preventing physicians and other health service providers from using interventions that are not established by outcome research as cost-effective. As the increased cost of health ser-vices has become recognized as one of the United States' most serious social problems, cost-containment efforts of government health care financing programs have intensified in ways that include effects on social work in health care services. Consequently, a variety of charac-teristics of health service organizations tend to constrain the role and function of the social workers that practice in them. The challenge for social workers is to find ways to adapt that will maximize their efficiency and effectiveness for the sake of all concerned-patient and family, organization, and funding source (Cowles, 2000).

The literature reviewed since 1967 to 2000 shows that there have been no change in the way social workers are perceived by phy-sicians, nurses, patients and administrators in hospital settings. To date, there has been no empirical research conducted on the percep-tions of doctors and nurses of the social work role in the emergency room. There is a need for social work practitioners and the profession to clarify social work roles to doctors and nurses in the medical emer-gency room.

CHAPTER FOUR

Theoretical Framework

Crisis intervention and Role theory were selected to help explain the role of the social worker in the emergency room. Social **work** in the emergency room is non- traditional specialty that involves working with physicians and nurses, who have been traditionally more attuned to illness and trauma than to patients' social needs (Elliot, 1987). Like other emergency room professionals, the social worker contributes to the overall effectiveness of the emergency room.

Social work in the emergency room is about working with physicians, nurses and other medical staff, in a collaborative way. It also deals with issues of crisis, such as sudden death, domestic violence, child abuse, elderly abuse, homelessness, chronic illness, substance abuse, alcohol abuse, as well as with issues of discharge planning.

The theories presented in this section provide a foundation for the research questions on which this study is based. Crisis intervention theory is important because patients enter the emergency room in crisis. Role theory provides a method of description and analysis of the behavior of people in organizations.

Crisis Theory

During the 1 950's and 1 960's, ego psychologists such as Allport, Maslow, and Erikson worked in the development of the philosophical base for crisis theory (Golan, 1978). Prior to this time, Hippocrates, a medical doctor, stated, "crisis is a sudden cessation of a state which gravely endangers life" (Golan, 1978).

Crisis intervention has been used to assist survivors of assault, families in turmoil, disaster victims, hospital emergency room patients, telephone hot lines callers, mental health emergency clients, individuals contemplating suicide, and couples experiencing difficulties (Poindexter, 1997).

During the early part of the twentieth century. several concerned groups formed suicide preventive centers such as The National Save a Life League in New York City, to assist people who were experiencing a crisis in their life. Although other centers like this existed elsewhere, they were few in number due to the lack of information regarding crisis intervention (Hendricks, 1991). In the 1960s social scientists pioneers such as Caplan (1964), Lindemann (1965), Parad (1965), and Rapoport (1965) developed seminal crisis theory and crisis intervention techniques (Poindexter, 1997).

The Social Work Dictionary (Barker, 1995) describes crisis as a term used by social workers in two ways:

1. An internal experience of emotional changes and distress.
2. A disastrous event that disrupts some essential functions of existing social institutions.

When seen as a period of emotional distress, a crisis is considered to be precipitated by a perceived life problem or to pose an obstacle to an important goal resulting in internal discord because the individual's typical strategies are inadequate. The outcome of the crisis can be positive if the individual eventually finds new coping mechanisms to deal with the unfamiliar event, thus adding to the repertoire of effective adaptive responses (Barker, 1995).

Traditional psychotherapy, as well as traditional psychoanalysis, is based primarily on the medical model and makes the assumption that the treatment took place because the patient had a disorder and required the expert knowledge of the "treater," that is doctor. The assumption was that anyone in psychological distress required specialized treatment to cure an illness by altering a defective personality (Rubin & Bloch, 1999). Crisis can cause severe psychological distress to any personality, wholesome or not. Crisis is a time of great vulnerability that can act as a fulcrum, allowing any intervention to carry a great deal of weight positive or negative (Rubin & Bloch, 1999). A state of active crisis exists if customary coping responses are unsuccessful, causing anxiety and uncertainty (Caplan, 1964; Golan, 1978; Parad, 1965; Rapoport, 1965, 1970).

Crisis theory is defined as a group of related concepts pertaining to people's reactions when confronted with new and unfamiliar experiences. These experiences may come in the form of natural disasters, significant loss, and changes in social status, and life cycle. This theory suggests that when people experience situations as crisis, they tend to follow predictable patterns of response (Barker, 1995; Rubin & Bloch, 1999).

Crisis theory has been strongly influenced by large body of research on human stress (Golan, 1987; Parad & Parad, 1990; Hendricks, 1991). Crisis intervention theory has grown out of concern for people who experience temporary feelings of acute distress leading to them being overwhelmed or unable to cope with life transitions and major stressful events. Although crisis theory is frequently cited as the basis for the broad range of environmental interventions and strategies widely used by social workers, there appears to be gaps in the knowledge base for practice, especially in the emergency room. Crisis intervention as a technique had its origin following the Coconut Grove fire in Boston in 1944, from the observations of the emotional difficulties that fire victims and their families had experienced with the catastrophe and its consequences. Health care professionals recognized the psychological aspects of crisis and began to develop strategies for intervention (Parad, 1965). Caplan (1964, 1974) emphasized the critical role of environmental resources in resolution and subsequent adaptation. Crisis intervention as defined by Rapoport (1965, 1970) is particularly relevant for social workers that encounter many of their clients in the emergency room facing trauma with stress and anxiety. Crisis intervention is the therapeutic practice used in helping clients in crisis to promote effective coping that can lead to positive growth and change by acknowledging the problem, recognizing its impact, and learning new or more effective behaviors for coping with similar predictable experiences (Barker, 1995).

In crisis intervention, the dynamics of the crisis are used in helping patients achieve a new balance of internal and external defenses, and support that permits them optimal functioning (Parad, 1965). In the emergency room, the primary role of the social worker involves crisis intervention. The social worker looks for the underlying causes of the presenting problem, meaning what happened in the patient's life that has caused a crisis. Whatever the nature of the crisis that speeds an emergency room visit — whether its is a sudden illness, exacerbation of chronic illness, failure of psychological defenses, a collapse of social supports, or abuse — the patient has come to the emergency room for immediate relief For that reason, the patient's motivation is frequently at a heightened level. Staff can act on the premise that this is the time when acting appropriately can make a difference in a person's life.

The need exists to help people whose crisis arises within the context of severe and chronic environmental stress. Providing appropriate interventions for people undergoing severe distress is part of everyday practice for most practitioners (Ell, 1995). Because there are psychological sequel deriving from a physical injury, and crisis intervention theory provides a basis for social work training and intervention, crisis intervention is a legitimate concern of social workers. It is important that the other professionals in the emergency room be apprised of the social workers' skills in crisis intervention. If patients are to be treated adequately, aspects of commutative experience can be realized.

Social workers in the health care field have long been aware that a person's management of crisis and stress can have an effect on health maintenance. People who feel more in control and more hopeful often seem to adjust better emotionally and feel better physically. Just as a crisis is seen as a danger and opportunity, crisis intervention validates difficulties and strengths simultaneously (Poindexter, 1997).

Role Theory

Several studies have indicated that social workers in hospital settings experience different expectations and perceptions of their role-sets that conflict with those of the social work profession and social workers' self-definition (Carrigan, 1974; Cowles & Lefcowits, 1975; Davidson, 1990).

The concept of "role" can be applied to interaction within the system, but also serves as a transactional or bridging concept between the individuals and the larger social systems in which they are operating. Roles are concerned with the expected behavior of a person occupying a particular social status or position in a social system (Campton & Galaway, 1989). The concept of "role" has been found to be both conceptually and practically useful as a construct, enabling the social science investigator to analyze the structure and functioning of social systems and to explain the behavior of individuals within such systems (Gross, et al., 1958; Merton, 1957; Davdison, 1990).

Merton (1957) defined a role as the behavioral enacting of the patterned expectations attributed to a particular social status. A status is a particular position in a system of relations. Status and role connect the culturally established expectations to sets of relationship that comprise a social structure. Three related concepts relating to role are the notions of role set, role complementary, and role conflict (Compton & Galaway, 1989).

For Merton (1957), individuals occupy "role sets," that is constellations of socially prescribed identities and expectations that are associated with a given social status. Those role-sets are embedded in a system of social relations and differential expectations. In the work environment of this study, the major roles are of social workers, physicians, and nurses.

The role-set of the social worker is achieved through professional socialization and certification (Compton & Galaway, 1989). The education and training for the performance of a professional role is a form of secondary socialization. Primary socialization occurs during childhood and forms fundamental aspects of a person's identity, such as gender roles, ethnicity, race, and class. Secondary socialization builds on primary socialization and is related to the formation of specific role-sets an individual occupies and is related to the formation of specific role-sets an individual occupies.

Important to the notion of role complementary and reciprocity is the fact that role position or statuses are usually paired (Compton & Galaway, 1989). If a system is to enjoy some stability and integration, there must be some reciprocity of expectations between role partners. Role conflict, according to Merton (1957), and Davidson (1990), takes two major forms: status strain and role strain. Merton (1957) refers to status as role conflict. Role conflict occurs when there are different perceptions by social workers of their roles and role perceptions of physicians and nurses of the social workers' role in the emergency room.

The second major form of the role conflict is that of role strain which is the subjective experience of a person who is having difficulty performing that role (Davidson, 1990) There are several forms of role strain. For example, role overload is when people feel that their role is too demanding. Some roles are vaguely defined, which can result in role-ambiguity. When roles are vaguely defined, they can result in role ambiguity. When roles are vaguely articulated, the actors experience strain because they do not know how much is expected of them (Davidson, 1990; Oberhofer & Simon. 1990).

According to Compton & Galaway (1989) the following concepts from the role theory are important to social workers:

- Certain behaviors are prescribed (buy us and by other elements of our social system) relative to our position within that system.
- Every role involves both our own expectations and abilities and those of one or more people.
- The notion of role expectations implies that there are certain social norms that set the outside limits for congruent, non- conflicted interactions and transactions between positions within the system and between positions within the system and between systems.

- There are emotionally charged value judgements to how people carry out their roles both on the part of the person occupying the role position and others.
- The concept of role, role functioning, role expectations, and role transactions may be used to increase the knowledge base used for the assessment of the problem situation.

The major function of physicians and nurses in hospitals is to care for patients' medical needs. Social work is thought to be an ancillary function. It may be that the restrictions on the activities of the social workers represent a contradiction between authority of expertise and legal authority in which the medical staff wish to hold power and dole it out to non-medical professional personnel. This may prevent social workers from encroaching on what they view as their right to determine the disposition of patients, even in areas where social workers may have greater expertise. For example, social workers tend to think of psychosocial problems as a social work arena. Yet, physicians and nurses increasingly perceive psychosocial problems as appropriate to their domain (Cowles & Lefcowitz, 1995; Cowles, 2000). If this were the case, the emergency room physicians, upon sensing that a patient had emotional problems would probably consult with a psychiatrist, who is also a medical doctor, instead of the social worker. even though the psychological disposition might be related to environmental problems or reaction to physical trauma. This means that social workers cannot expect to enter the organization and do their job as they envision it from their professional education.

Instead, they must be aware that their role definition is dependent on the cooperation and tacit (implied) consent of other professionals in the organization, who may or may not perceive their own roles as including some of what social workers think, is theirs (Cowles, 2000).

The discrepancy between the self-ascribed roles and functions of hospital social workers and those assigned by others has existed since the beginning of the profession. Social work formally entered hospitals in the United States at the invitation of Dr. Richard Cabot, Chief of Medicine at Massachusetts General Hospital in Boston, in

1905 (Davidson. 1990). The role of the first social worker was similar to that of an '"almoner." who was brought in to assess who was worthy of receiving alms in the form of health care in England. The early social workers were interested in providing services to those in need, but hospitals wanted them only to assess need for medical relief and to prevent abuse from the hospital (Davison, 1990). This discrepancy of roles is yet to be resolved; for health care social workers in the 2000s diagnostic related groups (DRG), managed care and other fiscal constrains call for functions quite different from those social workers would choose.

As pointed out by Davidson (1990), and Cowles (2000), hospital social work has developed a font of knowledge and has influenced patient care by promoting recognition of the psychosocial component of health care. Social workers in health care settings bring a person or family-centered model of care to assessment and treatment, which differs from the patient-focused medical model. To continue the progress achieved to date, social workers must continue to redefine their roles within the changing, financially oriented health care environment, while simultaneously preserving their social work values, knowledge skills, and ethics.

CHAPTER FIVE

Methodology

Introduction

This chapter describes the research design, data collection, instrumentation, and data analysis for the study. The primary focus of this study is to explain the procedures used to empirically test the hypothesis that doctors and nurses in the emergency room are more likely to perceive social worker's role as one that provide" concrete rather than clinical services. Social workers are more likely to perceive their role as one that provides both, concrete and clinical services.

Research Design

Research designs are strategic plans that define systematic methods to study research hypotheses or questions derived from theory or practice (MacEachron, 1995). This type of study falls under the rubric of descriptive research. In exploratory studies, the researcher seeks to describe an existing phenomenon (Rubing & Bubbie, 1997). The descriptive aspect of this study is that the researcher examined how doctors and nurses perceived the role of the social worker in the emergency room. In addition, the relationship between emergency room settings and perceptions of social workers' role in the emergency room was examined.

Several studies about health care professionals and expectations of social work role in hospital settings from 1967 through 2000 were reviewed (Olsen & Olsen, 1967; McCulloch & Brown, 1970; Phillips, et al., 1971; Cowles & Lefcowitz, 1992; Carrigan, 1974; Koeske, Koeske, & Mallinger, 1993; Egan & Kadushin, 1995; Auslander & Schneidman, 1996; McNeil et al., 1998; Cowles, 2000; Auslander, 2000). These studies showed that social workers define their function broadly, focusing on the whole person and including the patient, hospital, and community in professional decisions. Social workers in hospital settings are utilized for a narrow range of services that minimally use their skills. Doctors, nurses, and patients alike have been found to have more narrow views of social workers as "gofers" (Cowles & Lefcowitz, 1992).

For years we have taken as a forgone conclusion the notion that social work functions are best performed by a social work department within the hospital (Auslander, 2000). But in more than a few places around the world, this logic is being questioned. So that not too long ago, in Great Britain, the organizational responsibility for social work in hospitals was moved out of hospitals and into local communities, that is the social welfare system (Ranchman, 1997). Because hospital-based social work typically has not been income generating, social work departments have been vulnerable to downsizing and eliminated. In numerous hospitals around the world, social work departments, as discrete organizational entities, are being downsized or eliminated and the social workers dispersed throughout the institution (Arndt & Duchemin, 1995; Rizzo & Abrams, 2000). And in Australia, social work departments in some states are having to show that the services they offer cannot be provided better and more economically by other organizations in a process known as "competitive neutrality" (NAHCC, 1997). Social workers are being challenged to demonstrate how their services contribute to the mission of the organization.

As the increased cost of health services has become recognized as one of the United States' most serious social problems, cost-containment efforts of government health care financing programs have intensified in ways that include effects on social work in health care services. Consequently, a variety of characteristics of health service organizations tend to constrain the role and function of the social workers that practice in them. The challenge for social workers is to find ways to adapt that will maximize their efficiency and effectiveness for the sake of all concerned-patient and family, organization, and funding source (Cowles, 2000).

The literature reviewed since 1967 to 2000 shows that there have been no change in the way social workers are perceived by physicians, nurses, patients and administrators in hospital settings.

The study questions that guided this study include:

1. What are the differences in perceptions among social workers, doctors, and nurses regarding social workers' role in the medical emergency room.
2. Is there a difference in role perceptions between municipal and voluntary hospitals? by social workers.
3. How can social work education better address the need for the social worker's presence in the emergency room?

The study examined the following hypotheses:

I) Perceptions of the social workers' role in the medical emergency room will vary significantly by profession: Medicine, Nursing, and Social Work.

    a) Physicians and nurses are more likely to perceive social workers' role as one that provides concrete rather than clinical services.

    b) Social workers will perceive their role as providing both, concrete and clinical services.

II) There will be no significant differences between doctors and nurses in their perception of social workers' role in the emergency room by type of hospital (municipal or voluntary).

Concepts and Key Terms

In measuring values, beliefs, attitudes and perceptions the study attempts to objectify, in a quantifiable manner, attributes that are private, subjective and qualitative by nature. In this study, it was necessary to develop an instrument that would objectively and quantitatively measure the subjective perceptions of professional persons in term of their perceptions of the role of the social worker in the emergency room.

A person studying perceptions is asking how the world looks to the perceiver. He must look at how things appear to people not how they actually are, (Carrigan, 1974).

He must report not the character of the things that are perceived but the character of the perception, not the world that is experienced but the experience of that world as dependent upon experiencing organism. He does not merely observe; he observes observation. (Allport, 1955). P.23.

In order to provide a basis for universal discourse, terms relevant to the research study and the research variables must be defined. According to Rubin and Babbie (1997), a conceptual definition specifies precisely what is meant by a particular term by spelling out a set of indicators used to determine the qualitative category of a particular variable. Conceptualizing the study's terms and variables is the focus of this section.

Social worker is defined as a graduate of a school of social work with a master's degree, who uses his/her knowledge and skills to provide social services for clients (who may be individuals, families, groups, communities, organizations, or society in general). Social workers help people increase their capacities for problem solving and coping and they help obtain needed resources, facilitate interactions between individuals and influence social policies (Barker, 1995).

Role refers to behavioral enacting of the patterned expectations attributed to a particular social status (Merton, 1957).

Social worker's role refers to the legitimate and mandated activities social workers are expected by the organization to perform in relation to other members of emergency room staff and administration of the hospital, patients, outside agencies. and other services providers (Barker, 1995).

Perceptions of social workers' role refer to peoples' ideas of the valid and legitimate activities to be performed by social workers. Perceptions of social workers' role will be operationalized through a survey of opinions about the activities that social workers should engage in the emergency room.

Physician refers to a licensed practitioner of medicine, who has graduated from a college of medicine or osteopathology (Barker, 1995).

Registered nurse refers to a graduate nurse who has been legally licensed to practice after examinations by a state board of nurse examiners or similar regulatory authority, and who is legally entitled to use the designation RN (Barker. 1995).

Hospital type refers to the ownership and auspice of the hospital. Municipal hospitals in this study are those government entities run by the city of New York. Volunteer hospitals are those hospitals that are not for-profit and under the auspices of religious institutions. and universities.

For this study, municipal and volunteer hospitals were the settings for selecting the sample.

Description of the Setting

Descriptions of the sample hospitals and of social workers, doctors, and nurses who provided the data are presented below.

A total of 20 hospital medical emergency rooms participated in the study: Four from each Borough. Of these, ten were Municipal and ten were Voluntary (not for profit). For-profit hospitals were excluded from this study.

All available social workers, doctors and registered nurses, from all shifts assigned to the medical emergency rooms in each of the 20 participating hospitals were invited to participate in the study by the Directors of Social Work and Emergency Department of that hospital. This was done either at a staff meeting or through a memo to the staff. The sample population is unknown. There were 117 responses with an estimated rate of returns of 65%.

Sample Description

The sample included social workers, doctors, and registered nurses in hospital medical emergency rooms in New York City area. Psychiatric emergency rooms were excluded. Convenience sampling procedures were utilized. The strategy used for sampling was to select hospitals administrators' first and then use all eligible social workers, doctors, and nurses in each hospital medical emergency room (letters in appendix). The hospitals that participated in the study were selected from the 1998-1999 edition of the American Hospital Association Guide from which a list of all New York City acute care member hospitals was compiled. There were 24 municipal and voluntary hospitals on the list. Twenty of the hospitals' administrators contacted agreed to support their staffs participation in the study with written and verbal agreement. The hospitals ranged in size from 425 to 890 beds.

When a Director of Social Work or Emergency Room Department expressed willingness to have his/her staff participate in the study, the researcher met with that director to work out arrangements for the collection of the data and the initial presentation of the research to the staff In a few instances, these arrangements were worked out over the telephone. A time and place for data collection was arranged at each hospital emergency room. Upon receipt of consent, the researcher prepared packets including a cover letter, informed consent form, along with research questionnaire and self-addressed envelopes that were delivered in person to a designated employee in a participating hospital emergency room. Each potential respondent was given a packet. The cover letter explained the purposes of the research, the nature of the respondent's participation, the rights of confidentiality of persons involved in scientific research.

The designated employee (who was determined in consultation with the emergency room administrator) handed a survey questionnaire to the potential respondent with a brief statement about the respondent's cooperation in conducting the study. The respondents were asked to take 10 to 15 minutes of their time to complete the questionnaire and returned to the designated employee when finished.

Heading Instrument Items

These were selected from Carrigan's (1974) instrument, because they showed the divisions of concrete and clinical services.

Examples of items from each of the social worker's role sectors included are:

Concrete Services

The social worker should...
- Determine eligibility of patients for social services
- Help patients obtain medical appliances
- Interpret patients' feelings to physicians
- Report patients' medical problems to physicians
- Report patients' medical symptoms to physicians
- Explain physicians' orders to patients
- Act as liaison between doctor and patients
- Strengthen patients' participation in their own care
- Encourage patients to follow medical recommendations
  Interpret hospital services to community agencies
- Organize ex-patient groups to improve hospital resources
  Conduct pre-discharge study of homes
- Provide post-hospital employment counseling to patients
- Refer patients to community agencies

Clinical Services

The social worker should...
- Collaborate with other professionals on plan for patients' care
- Diagnose social problems of patients
- Determine patients' need for social services
- Recommend treatment for mentally ill
- Help patients overcome personal crisis
- Provide emotional support to patients
- Help patients adjust to illness
- Use psychotherapeutic techniques with patients

- Provide psychotherapy to emotionally disturbed patients
- Give consultation to other professionals on social problems of patients
- Orient allied health professionals about social work services
- Orient residents about social services

Even though distinctions between concrete and clinical services were made, concrete services require clinical skills that social workers have.

The complete set of 49 items may be found in the data collection package.

This list of activities was then used to collect empirical information regarding the perceptions that social workers, doctors, and nurses hold on the role of the social worker in the emergency room.

Measures

Independent Variable

The major independent variables are the disciplines of professionals in the emergency room (social worker, doctor, and nurse).

Dependent Variable

The major dependent variables are the respondents' perceptions of the various roles that social workers perform in the emergency room.

Operational Definitions And Measurements

Perception entails awareness, understanding and apprehension. According to Allport (1955), "it is that process by which organizations gain an understanding of, and a basis for reaching to, the world in which we live." A phenomenological experience of an object, that is to say, the way some object or situation appears to the subject, as dependent upon his own organism, as observer involved, non- denotative and 'private', is called percept (Allport, 1955). P.23.

Instrumentation

A questionnaire was developed based upon Carrigan's (1974) survey of hospital workers' perception of social work practice in health care settings. The original survey consisted of 1 00 activities performed by social workers in health settings. The items were analyzed and categorized in four areas: (a) Mediation between patients and organization (30 items); (b) Counseling (30 items); (c) Mediation between the patient and community (30 items); and (d) Administration (15 items). A typical mediation between the patient and the organization was, "The social worker educates the patient about hospital services." A typical counseling activity was, "The social worker screens patients for psychiatric evaluations." A typical mediation between patients and the community was, "The social worker locates aftercare facilities and placements for patients." A typical administrative activity was, "The social worker orients residents about social work services."

Carrigan's instrument was considered to be the most appropriate for this study because it was more extensive and complete than the others that were reviewed. Carrigan (1974) examined factors that might affect professional perceptions of the social work role, such as the degree of professional contact with social workers or professional orientation to social work. Her study was conducted in two Veteran's Administration hospitals associated with medical and social work schools.

Each item was included on two scales, the Perception Scale and the Actual Scale. The Perception Scale was anchored to a six-point response mode as follows: This activity should be performed 1) almost always by social workers, 2) mostly by social workers, 3) about equally by social workers and others, 4) mostly by other persons, 5) almost always by other persons, and 6) by no person in this setting. Actual Scale used the same response modes, but with the following stem: "This activity is actually performed": For scaling purposes, the above response modes were reversed coded so that 4=2, 2=4, 1=5. Items were summed for each scale.

In this study, 49 of the 100 items developed by Carrigan (1974) were determined by the researcher to be appropriate to the functions of the social worker in the medical emergency room. For example, one item on Carrigan's list is "The social worker helps patients with pre-admissions arrangements, which, since patients enter the emergency room on an emergency basis, would not be an emergency room social worker function. The items were organized as follows: Mediation between patient and organization (10 items); Counseling (10 items); Mediation between patient and community (11 items); and Administration (10 items).

The criteria that was used for the selection of questions was based on clinical and concrete services provided by social workers.

Reliability and Validity of the Instrument

Reliability of an instrument is defined as the consistency and stability of measurement (Rubin & babbie, 1997). There are two methods of measuring the reliability of an instrument: 1) Inter-observer and 2) Test-Retest.

To establish reliability and validity of the instrument, Carrigan (1974) began with a list of 167 items derived from a review of the literature on social work in health care settings. The items were then reviewed by health care social workers that practiced in health care settings. The list was evaluated by two panels, one of nurses and one of social workers, for clarity of the concepts, specificity of the items, and similarity among items. On the basis of the judgments, items were revised to increase clarity for a classification into groups. The ratings resulted in the elimination of items based on the criteria of moderate specificity and high clarity.

Carrigan (1974) tested the Perception and Actual Social Work Activity Scales for consistency over time; test-retest correlation for the total sample was .71 (range .53 to.90); for the psychologists, it was .69 (range .53 to .81), and for social workers, Carrigan cited Garret (1974) as suggesting that for small samples of narrow ranges, a consistency coefficient of between .50 and .60 is sufficient stability over time.

Carrigan (1974) employed the Test-Retest method for determining reliability. One of the disadvantages of this method is that the results are affected by differences in the conditions of administration and personal variations. Some of the factors that influence variations are: a) variations in the test situation, b) changes in the respondents, c) variations in the technique of the administrator, d) variations in the environment.

However, since homogeneity of content is not required to obtain a high level of reliability and due to time constraints, the Test-Retest method was selected. The mean scores for both tests were computed and they were similar with only small differences in the standard deviations. The results of this test showed that the instrument has a moderate to-high level of reliability. Furthermore, the repetition of this study by this author and the projected results will further establish the reliability of the instrument.

Validity refers to the extent to which an empirical measure adequately reflects to the real meaning of the concept under consideration (Rubin & Babbie, 1997). Carrigan (1974) considered the intricate and repeated winnowing and reconstruction of the final questionnaire, and also relied on the judgements of the various panels to establish content validity of the instrument.

Construct Validity refers to the degree to which a measure relates to other variables as expected within a system of theoretical relationship (Rubin and Babbie, 1997). Carrigan (1974), correlating sub-scales with total scores assessed construct validity for the Actual activities and with the difference of scores between Actual and Perceived activities. The two hospitals in the study were assessed separately. For both hospitals, sub-scale-total scale correlations for the Actual Scale were uniformly high, ranging from .69 to .93 (Mdn=. 87) for hospital I and from .61 to .81(Mdn=. 73) for hospital II.

Construct Validity was obtained by Carrigan (1974) by having the items on the questionnaire revised by a panel of experts. This panel consisted of three groups of professionals who helped to select the items of the questionnaire, review and revised the instrument. The first panel consisted of two VA Social Work Administrators for completeness of the universe of social work functions selected in the instrument and for the appropriateness of the language. Then, a panel of social workers were asked to rate a list of over 167 functional tasks related to medical social work in VA hospitals for specificity, generality, clarity, ambiguity and similarity. The instrument was reviewed for a third time by a panel of social workers with teaching, medical social work or VA hospital experience for the standardization process. Social work items and functions were categorized into broad categories. Also the panel checked the language of the instrument and finalized the comprehensive list of all social work functions to be included in the study.

These findings suggest that the individual factors are consistently related to a central construct. It would be expected that the subscale-scale correlations for the Actual Scale would be higher than the Perceived Scale, since the Actual Scale assessed self-reported actual behaviors, while the Perceived Scale assessed respondents' perceptions of "ought", which are more fluid than self-reports of actual behaviors.

The correlations of Actual Score and Perceived Score were .76 and .45, respectively for Hospital I, and .66 and .28, respectively for Hospital II. This means that the Actual Scores increased differences between Actual Scores and Perceived Scales Scores can be accounted for primarily by the difference in self-reported behaviors. That is, there was a consensus among social workers and psychologists about social work activities, and the differences could be accounted for by practice differences.

For Actual Hospital I, Actual Subscales, the range of correlations with the Perceived Scale total score was from .10 to .27. For Hospital II, Actual Scale, the total score was from. 19 to .55. These findings indicate that social work practice more closely approximated the perception of what social workers should do in hospital II than in hospital I. Indeed, as noted above, the Actual and Perceived Score correlations were higher in hospital II than in hospital I, which supports this observation. The findings suggest that the Actual and Perceived Scales of Carrigan's (1974) instrument have reasonable reliability and validity. They are consistent over time and they appear to measure both self-reported behaviors and perceptions of what social workers ought to be doing in hospitals in a valid way. The findings indicated that self-reports had less error than perceptions of oughtness, and that there was a consensus about which activity social workers should perform, and that variation in differences could be accounted for by differences in actual practice. All these findings suggest that the scales in Carrigan's (1974) instrument are reliable and valid. Thus, this author can conclude that the instrument selected for the study has a high degree of construct validity.

Content Validity refers to the degree to which a measure covers the range of meanings included within the concept (Rubin and Babbie, 1997). To compute this measurement Carrigan (1974) divided the questionnaire into four main categories and subscales A and B. Validity was obtained by the use of inter-correlations between subscale scores and the total scores for the instrument. It was found that the subscales correlated highly with the total scores on both scales A and B. Thus one can conclude that the instrument has a high degree of content validity.

Face Validity refers to that quality of an indicator that makes it seem a reasonable measure of some variables, Rubin and Babbie, (1997). Face validity for the instrument was obtained for the design of the questionnaire. The purpose of this author is to study differences in the opinion of the perception of the role of the social worker in the hospital emergency room among social workers, doctors, and nurses. The instrument consists of 49 questions listing all the possible services and tasks that the social worker should perform. It is fairly comprehensive and is divided into two main categories: clinical services and concrete services. The instrument has high face validity because it sets out to measure the perceptions of professionals about the role of the social worker in the emergency room and offers them an exhaustive list of services that can or are currently performed by social workers.

Several modifications were made in Carrigan's (1974) instrument for this study to increase ease of administration and validity. First, Carrigan began every item with "The social worker should." This construction was redundant and simply increased the length of the questionnaire. Therefore, the phrase, "The social worker should" was placed at the top of the list, and the rest of the item stem was included. This made the items and the questionnaire more easily readable.

A second modification was that the respondents limited the comparison with other persons. Instead, respondents focused on the extent to which the social worker should perform these functions. Respondents were asked to code their answers as follows:

1. **NEVER OR RARELY** done by social workers (5% of the time)
2. **SELDOM** done by social workers (about 25% of the time)
3. **SOMETIMES** done by social workers (50% of the time)
4. **OFTEN** done by social workers (about 75% of the time)
5. **ALWAYS OR NEARLY ALWAYS** done by social workers (95% of the time) This researcher thought that the comparison "with others" was confusing and that the point of the items was to find the extent to which social workers, doctors, and nurses thought that social workers carried out those functions.

Consent

This study was approved by the Yeshiva University Individual Review Board. Informal and written consent was requested from the directors of Social Work and directors of Emergency Room departments. Upon receipt of consent, each potential respondent was given a packet that included a cover letter explaining the purpose of the research, the nature of the respondent's participation, confidentiality, the rights of persons involved in scientific research, and informed consent form and a survey questionnaire that was given to a designated employee in a participating hospital emergency room. The respondents were asked to take 10 to 15 minutes of their time to complete the questionnaire and return it to the designated employee when finished.

Data Analysis

The purpose of the study was to determine the perceptions that social workers, doctors and nurses hold of the role of the social worker in the emergency room. This study also examined the relationship between the type of hospital, municipal vs. voluntary, and perceptions of social workers, doctors, and nurses about the role of the social worker in the emergency room. Data from returned questionnaires were entered into an electronic file preparation for the analysis.

The data were analyzed by computer, using a statistical package SPSS version (SPSS, 1999). The coding responses were collapsed into three categories: Never. Sometimes, and Always. Pearson's Chi-Square was used to compute the differences between expected observations (responses) among social workers, doctors, and nurses of the role of the social worker in the emergency room. Pearson's Chi-Square is a powerful statistical tool that assumes that the data is measured at the interval level (Rubing & Babbie, 1997). The hypotheses were tested in the null form; therefore. In order to disprove the null hypothesis, the .05 or lower level of significance was used.

Limitations of the Study

This study is limited to perceptions of social workers, doctors, and nurses about the role of the social worker in the medical emergency room. It is subject to the limitations of survey research. Although surveys are an important method to reliable and valid data from standardized instruments, they lack the ability to assess cultural meanings in the data. The items have been standardized to reduce bias so that the emergency room professionals interpret the items in the survey the same way.

A second limitation is that the respondents all participated voluntarily. Because the respondents were not randomly sampled from a defined population, but rather were selected at the convenience of the researcher, the representation of the sample was not verified, limiting the generalizability of the findings. Another limitation is that the population is unknown. The percentage of returned questionnaires can only be estimated.

CHAPTER SIX

Findings

This study was designed to determine if there are differences among doctors and nurses on the perceived role of social workers in the emergency room in municipal and voluntary hospitals. The perceptions were analyzed based on 49 items in a Likert- scale formatted questionnaire (See Appendix A). The data was first analyzed in the form of counts and were collapsed into three choices for each question. Later, the possible choices for each item were collapsed into three categories. Statistical significance was determined using the Pearson Chi-Square test. The rational for using the Chi-Square test was based on its appropriateness for this study; the data was nominal level.

The Chi-Square statistics measures the disparity between the observed frequencies. An examination of the formula to compute Chi-Square reveals that the value of the chi-square statistic increases as the disparity between the observed and the expected frequency increases. Hence, the larger the value of the tested statistic, the greater the evidence that the Null hypothesis is disproved. The decision was based to confirm or disconfirm the hypothesis based on the chosen level of statistical significance of .05 or less. The Null hypothesis disconfirmed at the probability level of less than or equal to .05.

The data was analyzed by computer, using a Statistical Package for Social Services (SPSS, 1999). Pearson's Chi-Square was used to compute the differences between observed and expected observations (responses) among social workers, doctors, and nurses of the role of the social worker in the emergency room.

The overall findings demonstrate that social workers perceive their role in the emergency rooms as providers of clinical and concrete services. On the other hand, doctors and nurses perceive the role of the social worker as providers of concrete services. Very little has changed between 1967 and now in the way doctors and nurses perceive the role of the social worker in hospital settings. This study is different in that it examined the perceptions that doctors, and nurses hold of the role of the social worker in the emergency room and comparing them with social workers' self perceptions of what they do.

Data Analysis

In this study, the researcher investigated the perceptions that doctors, and nurses hold of the role of the social worker in the emergency room and compared these views with social workers' self perceptions of what they do. In addition, this study examined the relationship between the type of hospital, voluntary vs. public, and perceptions of social workers, doctors, and nurses, of the role of the social worker in the emergency room. The data comes from 117 emergency room social workers, doctors, and nurses employed in 20 New York City metropolitan hospitals. The sample consisted of 38 social workers, 39 doctors, and 40 nurses. The independent variable is the type of professional in the emergency room (social worker, doctor, or nurse). The dependent variables are the respondents' perceptions of the various roles that social workers perform in the emergency room.

Demographics:

Years of Experience of Respondents

When the data was divided into two categories, municipal and voluntary, the result shows that more social workers from municipal hospitals (N=5) than social workers from voluntary hospitals (N=3) reported less than 3 years of emergency room experience. An equal proportion of social workers from municipal hospitals (N=6) and social workers from voluntary hospitals (N=6) reported 3 to 5 years of emergency room experience. More social workers from voluntary hospitals (N=8) than social workers from municipal hospitals (N=2) reported 11 to 15 years of emergency room experience. Only social workers from municipal hospitals (N=2) reported 16 or more years of emergency room experience. The result from the analysis shows some differences in years of experience between social workers from municipal and voluntary hospitals (see tables 1-1, 1-2). However, the difference in experience between social workers from municipal and voluntary hospitals was not statistically significant.

An equal proportion of doctors from municipal hospitals (N=4) and doctors from voluntary hospitals (N=4) reported less than 3 years of emergency room experience.

Doctors from municipal hospitals (N=3) and doctors from voluntary hospitals (N=2) reported 3 to 5 years of emergency room experience. Doctors from voluntary hospitals (N=10) and doctors from municipal hospitals (N=8) reported 6 to 10 years of emergency room experience. Only doctors from municipal hospitals (N=3) reported 11 to 15 years of emergency room experience. More doctors from voluntary hospitals (N=4) than doctors from municipal hospitals (N=1) reported 16 or more years of emergency room experience. The result from the analysis shows some difference of emergency room experience between doctors from municipal and voluntary hospitals. However, the difference in experience between doctors from municipal and voluntary hospitals was not statistically significant.

Nurses from voluntary hospitals (N=6) and nurses from municipal hospitals (N=4) reported less than 3 years of emergency room experience. More nurses from municipal hospitals (N=10) than nurses from voluntary hospitals (N=4) reported 3 to 5 years of emergency room experience. More nurses from voluntary hospitals (N=7) than nurses from municipal hospitals (N= 1) reported 6 to 1 0 years of emergency room experience. An equal proportion of nurses from municipal hospitals (N=3) and nurses from voluntary hospitals (N=3) reported 11 to 15 years of emergency room experience. Only nurses from municipal hospitals (N=2) reported 16 or more years of emergency room experience. The result from the analysis shows some difference of emergency room experience among nurses from municipal and voluntary hospitals. However, the difference in experience between nurses from municipal and voluntary hospitals was not statistically significant. See tables 1-1, 1-2

Age of Respondents

When the data was divided into two categories, municipal and voluntary, the result shows that only social workers from municipal hospitals (N=1) were less than 30 years old. Social workers from municipal hospitals (N=4) and social workers from voluntary hospitals (N=5) were 31 to 35 years old. Social workers from municipal hospitals (N=4) and social workers from voluntary hospitals (N=2) were 36 to 40 years old. Social workers from municipal hospitals (N=5) and social workers from voluntary hospitals (N=7) were 41 to 45 years old. Social workers from municipal hospitals (N=4) and social workers from voluntary hospitals (N=1) were 46 to 50 years old. Social workers from municipal hospitals (N=1) and social workers from voluntary hospitals (N=2) were 51 to 55 years old. The result from the analysis shows no statistically significant difference of age among social workers from municipal and voluntary hospitals. Only (N=1) doctors from municipal hospitals were less than 30 years old. Doctors from municipal hospitals (N=1) and doctors from voluntary hospitals (N=6) were 31-35 years old Id. Doctors from municipal hospitals (N=1) and doctors from voluntary hospitals (N=4) were 36-40 years old. Doctors from municipal hospitals (N=5) and doctors from voluntary hospitals (N=4) were 41-45 years old. Doctors from municipal hospitals (N=8) and doctors from voluntary hospitals (N=3) were 46-50 years old. An equal number of doctors from municipal hospitals (N=1) and doctors from voluntary hospitals (N=1) were 56-60 years old. Doctors from municipal hospitals (N=1) and doctors from voluntary hospitals (N=2) were 61 and older. The result from this analysis shows no significant difference of age among doctors from municipal and voluntary hospitals.

Only nurses from municipal hospitals (N=1) were less than 30 years old. More nurses from voluntary hospitals (N=5) than nurses from municipal hospitals (N=3) were 31-35 years old. Same amount of nurses from municipal hospitals (N=4) and nurses from voluntary hospitals (N=4) were 36-40 years old. Almost the same amount of nurses from municipal hospitals (N=5) and nurses from voluntary hospitals (N=4) were 41-45 years old. Almost the same amount of nurses from municipal hospitals (N=6) and nurses from voluntary hospitals (N=5) were 46-50 years old. Almost the same amount of nurses from municipal hospitals (N=1) and nurses from voluntary hospitals (N=2) were 51-55 years old. The result from this analysis shows no significant difference of age among nurses from municipal and voluntary hospitals. See tables 2-1, 2-2

Sex of Respondents

When the data was divided into two categories (tables 3-1 and 3-2), more social workers from voluntary hospitals (N=15) than social workers from municipal hospitals (N=10) were males. Whereas more social workers from municipal hospitals (N=9) than social workers from voluntary hospitals (N=4) were females. More doctors from municipal hospitals (N=12) than doctors from voluntary hospitals (N=3) were males. Whereas more doctors from voluntary hospitals (N=17) than doctors from municipal hospitals (N=7) were females. More nurses from municipal hospitals (N=18) than nurses from voluntary hospitals (N=2) were males. Whereas more nurses from voluntary hospitals (N=18) than nurses from municipal hospitals (N=2) were females. The result from the analysis shows a statistically significant difference of gender among professionals from both settings. See tables 3-1, 3-2.

Ethnic Background of Respondents

When the data was divided into two categories, municipal and voluntary (tables 4-1 and 4-2), the result shows that more social workers from voluntary hospitals (N=9) than social workers from municipal hospitals (N=7) reported to be White non-Hispanic. Social workers from municipal hospitals (N=4) and social workers from voluntary hospitals (N=3) reported to be Hispanic. An equal number of social workers from municipal hospitals (N=3) and voluntary hospitals (N=3) reported to be African American. More social workers from voluntary hospitals (N=6) than social workers from municipal hospitals (N=3) reported to be other.

When the data was divided into two categories, municipal and voluntary, the result shows that more doctors from municipal hospitals (N=9) than doctors from voluntary hospitals (N=2) reported to be White non-Hispanic. Doctors from municipal hospitals (N=6) and doctors from voluntary hospitals (N=5) reported to be Hispanic. Doctors from municipal hospitals (N=4) and doctors from voluntary hospitals (N=5) reported to be African-American. Only doctors from voluntary hospitals (N=8) reported to be other. (See tables 4-1 and 4-2). Though there were some differences in ethnic background between the respondents in municipal and voluntary hospitals, these differences were not statistically significant.

When the data was divided into two categories, municipal and voluntary, the result shows that more nurses (N=9) than nurses (N=1) reported to be White-non Hispanic. An equal proportion of nurses (N=4) from municipal and voluntary hospitals (N=4) reported to be Hispanic. More nurses (N=5) from voluntary hospitals than (N=3) nurses from municipal hospitals reported to be African-American. More nurses from municipal hospitals (N=10) than nurses from municipal hospitals (N=4) reported to be other. See tables 4-1, 4-2

Table 1-1

Years of emergency room experience
Frequencies and Percentages

Responses	Municipal social worker (N=19)		Municipal doctor (N=19)		Municipal nurse (N=20)		Total
	Freq	%	Freq	%	Freq	%	
Less than 3	5	26.3		21.1		20.0	13
3 to 5	6	31.6	3	15.8	10	50.0	19
6 to 10	4	21.1	8	42.1	10	5.0	13
11 to 15	2	10.5	3	15.8	3	15.0	8
16 more	2	10.5		5.3	2	10.5	5
Total	19	100.0	19	100.0	20	100.0	58

Chi-Square= 10.20 p<.24

Table 1-2

Years of emergency room experience.
Frequencies and Percentages

Responses	Municipal social worker (N=19)		Municipal doctor (N=19)		Municipal nurse (N=20)		Total
	Freq	%	Freq	%	Freq	%	
Less than 3	3	15.8	4	20.0	6	30.0	13
3 to 5	6	31.6	2	10.0	4	20.0	12
6 to 10	8	42.1	10	50.0	7	35.0	25
11 to 15	2	10.5			3	15.0	5
16 more			4	20.0			4
Total	19	100.0	20	100.0	20	100.0	59

Chi-Square= 14.3 p<.07

Table 2-1

Age of respondent.
Frequencies and Percentages

Responses	Municipal social worker (N=19)		Municipal doctor (N=19)		Municipal nurse (N=20)		Total
	Freq	%	Freq	%	Freq	%	
Less than 30	1	5.3	1	5.3		5.0	3
31 - 35	4	21.1	1	5.3	3	15.0	8
36 - 40	4	21.1	1	26.3	4	20.0	9
41 - 45	5	26.3	5	5.3	5	25.0	15
46 - 50	4	21.1	8	42.1	6	30.0	18
51 - 55	1	5.3	1	5.3	1	5.3	3
56 - 60			1	5.3			1
61 - over			1	5.3			1
Total	19	100.0	19	100.0	20	100.0	58
Chi-Square=9. 1 5 p<.82							

Table 2-2

Age of respondents.
Frequencies and Percentages

Responses	Municipal social worker (N=19)		Municipal doctor (N=19)		Municipal nurse (N=20)		Total
	Freq	%	Freq	%	Freq	%	
Less than 30							
31 - 35	5	30.0	6	26.3	5	25.0	16
36 - 40	2	10.0	4	21.1	4	20.0	10
41 - 45	7	35.0	4	21.1	4	20.0	15
46 - 50	1	5.0	3	15.8	5	25.0	9
51 - 55	2	10.0	1	5.3	2	10.0	5
56 - 60							
61 - over	2	10.0	2	10.5			4
Total	19	100.0	20	100.0	20	100.0	59

Chi-Square=?.08 p<.71

Table 3-1

Sex of respondent.
Frequencies and Percentages

Responses	Municipal social worker (N=19)		Municipal doctor (N=19)		Municipal nurse (N=20)		Total
	Freq	%	Freq	%	Freq	%	
Male	10	52.6	12	63.2	18	90.0	40
Female	9	47.4	7	36.8	2	10.0	18
Total	19	100.0	19	100.0	20	100.0	58
Chi-Square=6.80 p<.03							

Table 3-2

Sex of respondent.
Frequencies and Percentages

Responses	Municipal social worker (N=19)		Municipal doctor (N=19)		Municipal nurse (N=20)		Total
	Freq	%	Freq	%	Freq	%	
Male	15	80.0	3	15.8	2	10.0	21
Female	4	20.0	17	84.2	18	90.0	38
Total	19	100.0	20	100.0	20	100.0	59
Chi-Square=26.19 p<.00							

Table 4-1

Ethnic background of respondents.
Frequencies and Percentages

Responses	Municipal social worker (N=19)		Municipal doctor (N=19)		Municipal nurse (N=20)		Total
	Freq	%	Freq	%	Freq	%	
White non-Hispanic	9	47.4	9	47.4	9	45.0	27
Hispanic	4	21.1	6	31.6	4	20.0	14
African-American	3	15.8	4	21.1	3	15.0	10
Other	3	15.8			4	20.0	7
Total	19	100.0	19	100.0	20	100.0	58

Chi-Square=4.46 p<.61

Table 4-2

Ethnic background of respondents.
Frequencies and Percentages

Responses	Municipal social worker (N=19)		Municipal doctor (N=19)		Municipal nurse (N=20)		Total
	Freq	%	Freq	%	Freq	%	
White non-Hispanic	7	35.0	2	10.5		5.0	10
Hispanic	3	15.0	5	26.3	4	20.0	12
African-American	3	15.0	5	26.3	5	25.0	13
Other	6	35.0	8	36.8	10	50.0	24
Total	19	100.0	20	100.0	20	100.0	59

Chi-Square=7.54 p<.24

Survey Items

1. The first item in the survey analyzed was the degree to which social workers, doctors, and nurses in both settings agreed that the social worker should determine eligibility of patients for services in the emergency room. Table 1-1 shows this analysis.

Table 1-1

The social worker should determine eligibility of patients for social services.
Frequencies and Percentages

Responses	Municipal social worker (N=19)		Municipal doctor (N=19)		Municipal nurse (N=20)		Total
	Freq	%	Freq	%	Freq	%	
Never	24	63.2	39	100.0	40	100.0	103
Sometimes	8	21.1					8
Always	6	15.8					6
Total	38	100.0	39	100.0	40	100.0	117
Pearson Chi-Square=33.06 p<.01							

All the doctors (N=39) and nurses surveyed (N=40) agreed that the social worker should never determine eligibility of patients for social services. Although the majority of social workers (N= 24) also agreed that the social worker should never determine eligibility of patients for social services, they were less opposed to this than were the other group of professionals. One third (N=14) of all social workers agreed that they should play some role in determining the eligibility of patients for social services.

The difference in the perception of the role of the social worker in determining eligibility of social services among social workers, doctors, and nurses is statistically significant and the Null Hypothesis is rejected. Therefore the hypothesis that doctors and nurses are more likely to perceive the role of the social worker in the emergency room as providing concrete rather than clinical services was supported.

When the data was divided into two categories, municipal and voluntary, the result shows that more social workers from voluntary hospitals (N=19) than social workers from municipal hospitals (N=5) agreed that the social worker should never determine eligibility of patients for social services. All doctors and nurses from municipal (N=20) and voluntary hospitals (N=20) agreed that the social worker should never determine eligibility of patients for social services.

The difference in the opinion about determination of eligibility of social services among social workers, doctors, and nurses is statistically significant in both settings and the Null Hypothesis is rejected. Therefore, the hypothesis that there **will be** no significant differences between doctors and nurses in their perception of the social worker's role in the emergency room in both types of hospitals (municipal or voluntary) was supported. See tables 1-2, 1-3.

Table 1-2

The social worker should determine eligibility of patients for social services.
Frequencies and Percentages

Responses	Municipal social worker (N=19)		Municipal doctor (N=19)		Municipal nurse (N=20)		Total
	Freq	%	Freq	%	Freq	%	
Never	5	26.3	19	100.0	20	100.0	44
Sometimes	8	42.1					8
Always	16	31.6					6
Total	19	100.0	19	100.0	20	100.0	58
Pearson Chi-Square=33.06 p<.01							

Table 1-3

The social worker should determine eligibility of patients for social services.
Frequencies and Percentages

Responses	Municipal social worker (N=19)		Municipal doctor (N=19)		Municipal nurse (N=20)		Total
	Freq	%	Freq	%	Freq	%	
Never	19	100.0	20	100.0	20	100.0	59
Total	19	100.0	20	100.0	20	100.0	59
Pearson Chi-Square=37.88 p<.01							

2. The second item in the survey analyzed was the degree to which social workers, doctors, and nurses in both settings agreed that the social worker should help patients obtain medical appliances. Table 2-1 shows this analysis.

Table 2-1

The social worker should help patients obtain medical appliances.
Frequencies and Percentages

Responses	Municipal social worker (N=19)		Municipal doctor (N=19)		Municipal nurse (N=20)		Total
	Freq	%	Freq	%	Freq	%	
Never	13	34.2	3	7.7	4	10.0	20
Sometimes	25	65.8	36	92.3	36	90.0	97
Total	38	100.0	39	100.0	40	100.0	117
Pearson Chi-Square=11.7 p<.01							

A majority of social workers (N=25), doctors (N=36) and nurses (N=36) were in agreement that the social worker should sometimes help patients obtain medical appliances. However, a significantly larger number of social workers (N=13) compared to the number of doctors (N=3) and nurses (N=4) responded that the social worker should never help patients obtain medical appliances.

The difference in the perception of the role of the social worker in helping patients obtain medical appliances among social workers, doctors, and nurses was statistically significant and the Null Hypothesis was rejected. Therefore, the hypothesis that doctors and nurses are more likely to perceive the social worker's role in the emergency room as providing concrete services rather than clinical was supported.

When the data was divided into two categories, municipal and voluntary, the result shows that social workers from municipal hospitals (N=13) and social workers from voluntary hospitals (N=12) were in agreement that the social workers should sometimes help patients obtain medical appliances. Doctors from municipal hospitals (N=17) and doctors from voluntary hospitals (N=19) were in agreement that the social worker should sometimes help patients obtain medical appliances. Most nurses from municipal hospitals (N=19) and nurses from voluntary hospitals (N=17) were in agreement that the social worker should sometimes help patients obtain medical appliances.

The difference in opinions about helping patients obtain medical appliances among social workers, doctors, and nurses is statistically significant in both settings and the Null Hypothesis is rejected. Therefore, the hypotheses that there will be no significant differences between doctors and nurses in their perception of the social workers' role in the emergency room in both types of hospitals (municipal and voluntary) was supported. See tables 2-2, 2-3.

Table 2-2

The social worker should help patients obtain medical appliances. Frequencies and Percentages

Responses	Municipal social worker (N=19)		Municipal doctor (N=19)		Municipal nurse (N=20)		Total
	Freq	%	Freq	%	Freq	%	
Never	6	31.6	2	10.5	1	5.0	9
Sometimes	13	68.4	17	895	19	95.0	49
Total	19	100.0	19	100.0	20	100.0	58

Pearson Chi-Square=5.78 p<.05

Table 2-3

The social worker should help patients obtain medical appliances. Frequencies and Percentages

Responses	Municipal social worker (N=19)		Municipal doctor (N=19)		Municipal nurse (N=20)		Total
	Freq	%	Freq	%	Freq	%	
Never	7	36.8	1	5.0	3	15.3	11
Sometimes	12	63.2	19	95.0	17	85.0	48
Total	19	100.0	20	100.0	20	100.0	59

Pearson Chi-Square=6.77 p<.03

3. The third item analyzed in the survey was the degree to which social workers, doctors, and nurses from both hospitals agreed that the social worker should interpret feelings of patients to physicians. Table 3-1 shows this analysis.

Table 3-1

The social worker should interpret feelings of patients to physicians. Frequencies and Percentage

Responses	Municipal social worker (N=19)		Municipal doctor (N=19)		Municipal nurse (N=20)		Total
	Freq	%	Freq	%	Freq	%	
Never			4	10.3	2	5.0	6
Sometimes	13	34.2	17	43.6	15	37.5	45
Always	25	65.8	18	46.2	23	57.5	66
Total	38	100.0	39	100.0	40	100.0	117
Pearson Chi-Square=5.73 p<.22							

More social workers (N=25) and nurses (N=23) than doctors (N=188) were in agreement that the social worker should always interpret feelings of patients to physicians. Only doctors (N=4) and nurses (N=2) felt that the social worker should never interpret feelings of patients to physicians.

The difference in the perception of the role of the social worker in interpreting feelings of patients to physicians among social workers, doctors, and nurses was not statistically significant and the Null Hypothesis was accepted. Therefore, the hypothesis that doctors and nurses are more likely to perceive the role of the social worker in the emergency room as providing concrete rather than clinical services was not supported.

When the data was divided into two categories, municipal and voluntary, the result shows that more social workers from municipal hospitals (N=15) than social workers from voluntary hospitals (N=10) were in agreement that the social worker should interpret feelings of patients to physicians. More doctors from municipal hospitals (N=10) than doctors from voluntary hospitals (N=8) were in agreement that the social worker should interpret feelings of patients to physicians. Nurses from voluntary hospitals (N=12) and nurses from municipal hospitals (N=11) were in agreement that the social worker should interpret feelings of patients to physicians.

The difference in opinions about interpreting feelings of patients to physicians among social workers, doctors, and nurses was statistically significant in municipal hospitals only and the Null Hypothesis was accepted. Therefore, the hypothesis that there will be no significant differences among doctors and nurses in their perceptions of social workers' role in the emergency room in both types of hospitals (municipal and voluntary) was not supported. See tables 3-2. 3-3.

Table 3-2

The social worker should interpret feelings of patients to physicians. Frequencies and Percentages

Responses	Municipal social worker (N=19)		Municipal doctor (N=19)		Municipal nurse (N=20)		Total
	Freq	%	Freq	%	Freq	%	
Never			3	15.8	2	5.0	3
Sometimes	4	21.1	6	31.6	9	45.0	19
Always	15	78.9	10	52.6	11	55.0	36
Total	19	100.0	19	100.0	20	100.0	58
Pearson Chi-Square=9.18 p<.05							

Table 3-3

The social worker should interpret feelings of patients to physicians. Frequencies and Percentages

Responses	Municipal social worker (N=19)		Municipal doctor (N=19)		Municipal nurse (N=20)		Total
	Freq	%	Freq	%	Freq	%	
Never			1	5.0	2	10.0	3
Sometimes	9	47.4	11	55.0	6	30.0	26
Always	10	52.6	8	40.0	12	60.0	30
Total	19	100.0	20	100.0	20	100.0	59
Pearson Chi-Square=4.20 p<.37							

4. The fourth item analyzed in the survey was the degree to which the social workers, doctors, and nurses from both settings agreed that the social worker should report patients' medical problems to physicians. Table 4-1 shows this analysis.

Table 4-1

**The social worker should report patients' medical problems to physicians.
Frcquencies and Perccntage**

Responses	Municipal social worker (N=19)		Municipal doctor (N=19)		Municipal nurse (N=20)		Total
	Freq	%	Freq	%	Freq	%	
Never	6	15.8	6	15.4	4	10.0	16
Sometimes	25	65.8	17	43.6	15	37.5	57
Always	7	18.4	16	41.0	21	52.5	44
Total	38	100.0	39	100.0	40	100.0	117
Pearson Chi-Square= 10.31 p<.03							

Nearly all social workers (N=32), doctors (N=33) and nurses (N=36) agreed that the social worker should report patients' medical problems to physicians.

The difference in the perception of the role of the social worker about reporting patients' medical problems to physicians among social workers, doctors and nurses is statistically significant and the Null Hypothesis was rejected. Therefore, the hypothesis that doctors and nurses are more likely to perceive the role of the social worker in the emergency room as providing concrete rather than clinical services was supported.

When the data was divided into two categories, municipal and voluntary, the result shows that most social workers from municipal hospitals (N=17) and social workers from voluntary hospitals (N=15) agreed that the social worker should report medical problems of patients' to physicians. Doctors from municipal hospitals (N=15) and doctors from voluntary hospitals (N=18) were in agreement that the social worker should report patients' medical problems to physicians. All nurses from voluntary hospitals (N=20) and nearly all nurses from municipal hospitals (N=16) were in agreement that the social worker should report patients' medical problems to physicians.

The difference in opinions about reporting patients' medical problems to physicians among social workers, doctors, and nurses was statistically significant in voluntary hospitals only and the Null Hypothesis was accepted. Therefore, The hypothesis that there will be no significant differences among doctors and nurses in their perceptions of the social worker's role in the emergency room in both types of hospitals (municipal and voluntary) was not supported. See tables 4-1, 4-2.

Table 4-2

The social worker should report patients' medical problems to physicians.
Frequencies and Percentage

Responses	Municipal social worker (N=19)		Municipal doctor (N=19)		Municipal nurse (N=20)		Total
	Freq	%	Freq	%	Freq	%	
Never	2	10.5	4	21.1			6
Sometimes	12	63.2	8	42.1	11	55.0	31
Always	5	26.3.	7	36.8	9	45.0	21
Total	19	100.0	19	100.0	20	100.0	58
Pearson Chi-Square=5.92 p=<.20							

Table 4-3

The social worker should report patients' medical problems to physicians.
Frequencies and Percentages

Responses	Municipal social worker (N=19)		Municipal doctor (N=19)		Municipal nurse (N=20)		Total
	Freq	%	Freq	%	Freq	%	
Never	4	21.1	2	10.0	4	20.0	10
Sometimes	13	68.4	9	45.0	4	20.0	26
Always	2	10.5	9	45.0	12	60.0	23
Total	19	100.0	20	100.0	20	100.0	59
Pearson Chi-Square=12.45 p<.01							

5. The fifth item analyzed in the survey was the degree to which the social workers, doctors, and nurses from both settings agreed that the social worker should report patients' medical symptoms to physicians. Table 5-1 shows this analysis.

Table 5-1

The social worker should report patients' medical symptoms to physicians.
Frequencies and Percentages

Responses	Municipal social worker (N=19)		Municipal doctor (N=19)		Municipal nurse (N=20)		Total
	Freq	%	Freq	%	Freq	%	
Never	12	31.6	9	21.1	6	15.0	27
Sometimes	21	55.3	19	48.7	18	45.0	58
Always	5	13.2	11	28.2	16	40.0	32
Total	38	100.0	39	100.0	40	100.0	117
Pearson Chi-Square=7.89 p<.09							

The majority of social workers (N=26), doctors (N=30) and nurses (N=34) agreed that the social worker should always report patients' medical symptoms to physicians.

However, a significant number of social workers (N=12) compared to doctors (N=9) and nurses (N=6) responded that the social worker should never report patients' medical symptoms to physicians. The difference in the perception of the role of the social worker in reporting patients' medical symptoms to physicians among social workers, doctors, and nurses was not statistically significant and the Null Hypothesis was accepted. Therefore, the hypothesis that doctors and nurses are more likely to perceive the role of the social worker in the emergency room as providing concrete rather than clinical services was not supported.

When the data was divided into two categories, municipal and voluntary, the result shows that nearly all social workers from voluntary hospitals (N=14) and social workers from municipal hospitals (N=12) agreed that the social worker should report patients' medical symptoms to physicians. Most doctors from voluntary hospitals (N=16) and doctors from municipal hospitals (N=14) agreed that the social worker should report patients' medical symptoms to physicians. All nurses from municipal hospitals (N=20) and nearly most nurses from voluntary hospitals (N=14) agreed that the social worker should report patients' medical symptoms to physicians.

The difference in opinions about reporting patients' medical symptoms to physicians among social workers, doctors, and nurses is statistically significant in both settings and the Null Hypothesis was rejected. Therefore, the hypothesis that there will be no significant differences among doctors and nurses in their perceptions of social workers' role in the emergency room in both types of hospitals (municipal and voluntary) was supported. See tables 5-1, 5-2.

Table 5-2

The social worker should report patients' medical symptoms to physicians.
Frequencies and Percentages

Responses	Municipal social worker (N=19)		Municipal doctor (N=19)		Municipal nurse (N=20)		Total
	Freq	%	Freq	%	Freq	%	
Never	7	36.8	5	26.3			12
Sometimes	8	42.1	7	36.8	14	70.0	29
Always	4	21.1	7	36.8	6	30.0	17
Total	19	100.0	19	100.0	20	100.0	58
Pearson Chi-Square=10.13 p<.03							

Table 5-3

The social worker should report patients' medical symptoms to physicians.
Frequencies and Percentages

Responses	Municipal social worker (N=19)		Municipal doctor (N=19)		Municipal nurse (N=20)		Total
	Freq	%	Freq	%	Freq	%	
Never	5	26.3	4	20.0	6	30.0	15
Sometimes	13	68.4	12	60.0	4	20.0	29
Always		5.3	4	20.0	10	50.0	15
Total	19	100.0	20	100.0	20	100.0	59
Pearson Chi-Square=10.13 p<.03							

6. The sixth item analyzed in the survey was the degree to which the social workers, doctors, and nurses from both settings agreed that the social worker should explain physicians' orders to patients. Table 6-1 shows this analysis.

Table 6-1

The social worker should explain physicians' orders to patients.
Frequencies and Percentages

Responses	Municipal social worker (N=19)		Municipal doctor (N=19)		Municipal nurse (N=20)		Total
	Freq	%	Freq	%	Freq	%	
Never	14	36.8	10	25.6	11	27.5	35
Sometimes	17	44.7	16	41.0	15	37.5	48
Always	7	18.4	13	33.3	4	35.0	34
Total	38	100.0	39	100.0	40	100.0	117
Pearson Chi-Square=3.85 p<.49							

The majority of social workers (N=24), doctors (N=29), and nurses (N=29) agreed that the social worker should explain physicians' orders to patients. A significant number of social workers, (N=14), doctors (N=10), and nurses (N=11) agreed that the social worker should never explain physicians' orders to patients.

The difference in the perception of the role of the social worker in explaining physicians' orders to patients among social workers, doctors, and nurses was not statistically significant and the Null Hypothesis was accepted. Therefore, the hypothesis that doctors and nurses are more likely to perceive the role of the social worker in the emergency room as providing concrete rather than clinical services was not supported.

When the data was divided into two categories, municipal and voluntary, the result shows that most social workers from voluntary hospitals (N=11) and social workers from municipal hospitals (N=13) agreed that the social worker should explain physicians' orders to patients. Nearly all doctors from municipal hospitals (N=13) and doctors from voluntary hospitals (N=16) agreed that the social worker should explain physicians' orders to patients. Nearly all nurses from municipal hospitals (N=16) and nurses from voluntary hospitals (N=13) agreed that the social worker should explain physicians' orders to patients.

Nearly the same amount of social workers from municipal hospitals (N=8) and social workers from voluntary hospitals (N=6) agreed that the social worker should never explain physicians' orders to patients. Nearly the same amount of doctors from municipal hospitals (N=6) and doctors from voluntary hospitals (N=4) agreed that the social worker should never explain physicians' orders to patients. Nearly the same amount of nurses from municipal hospitals (N=4) and nurses from voluntary hospitals (N=7) agreed that the social worker should never explain physicians' orders to patients.

The difference in opinions about explaining physicians' orders to patients among social workers, doctors, and nurses was statistically significant in voluntary hospitals only and the Null Hypothesis was accepted. Therefore, the hypothesis that there will be no significant differences among doctors and nurses in their perception of the social workers' role in the emergency room in both types of hospitals (municipal and voluntary) was not supported. See tables 6-1, 6-2.

Table 6-2

The social worker should explain physicians' orders to patients. Frequencies and Percentages

Responses	Municipal social worker (N=19)		Municipal doctor (N=19)		Municipal nurse (N=20)		Total
	Freq	%	Freq	%	Freq	%	
Never	8	42.1	6		4	20.0	18
Sometimes	6	31.6	5	26.3	11	55.0	22
Always	5	26.3	8	42.1	5	25.0	18
Total	19	100.0	19	100.0	20	100.0	58

Pearson Chi-Square=5.07 p<.28

Table 6-3

The social worker should explain physicians' orders to patients. Frequencies and Percentages

Responses	Municipal social worker (N=19)		Municipal doctor (N=19)		Municipal nurse (N=20)		Total
	Freq	%	Freq	%	Freq	%	
Never	6	31.6	4	20.0	7	35.0	17
Sometimes	11	57.9	11	55.0	4	20.0	26
Always	2	10.5	5	25.0	9	45.0	16
Total	19	100.0	20	100.0	20	100.0	59

Pearson Chi-Square=9.17 p<.05

7. The seventh item analyzed in the survey was the degree to which the social workers, doctors, and nurses from both settings agreed that the social worker should act as liaison between doctor and patients. Table 7-1 shows this analysis.

Table 7-1

The social worker should act as liaison between doctor and patients. Frequencies and Percentages

Responses	Municipal social worker (N=19)		Municipal doctor (N=19)		Municipal nurse (N=20)		Total
	Freq	%	Freq	%	Freq	%	
Never			3	7.7	2	5.0	5
Sometimes	7	18.4	9	23.1	10	25.0	26
Always	31	81.6	27	69.2	28	70.0	86
Total	38	100.0	39	100.0	40	100.0	117
Pearson Chi-Square=3.64 p<.45							

All social workers (N=38, 100.0%), nearly all doctors (N=36), and nearly all nurses (N=38) agreed that the social worker in the emergency room should act as liaison between doctor and patients. Only a small number of doctors (N=3) and nurses (N=2) agreed that the social worker should never act as liaison between doctor and patients.

The difference in the perception of the role of the social worker in acting as liaison among doctor and patients among social workers, doctors, and nurses was not statistically significant and the Null Hypothesis was accepted. Therefore, the hypothesis that doctors and nurses are more likely to perceive the role of the social worker in the emergency room as providing concrete rather than clinical services was not supported.

When the data was divided into two categories, municipal and voluntary, the result shows that all social workers from municipal hospitals (N=19) and all social workers from voluntary hospitals (N=19) agreed that the social worker should act as liaison between doctor and patients. Nearly all doctors from municipal hospitals (N=17) and nearly all doctors from voluntary hospitals (N=19) agreed that the social worker should act as liaison between doctor and patients. All nurses from municipal hospitals (N=20) and nearly all nurses from voluntary hospitals (N=18) also agreed that the social worker should act as liaison between doctor and patients.

The difference in opinions about acting as liaison between doctor and patients among social workers, doctors, and nurses was not statistically significant in both settings and the Null Hypothesis was accepted. The hypothesis that there will be no significant differences among doctors and nurses in their perception of the social workers' role in the emergency room in both types of hospitals (municipal and voluntary) was not supported. See tables 7-2. 7-3.

Table 7-2

The social worker should act as liaison between doctor and patients. Frequencies and Percentages

Responses	Municipal social worker (N=19)		Municipal doctor (N=19)		Municipal nurse (N=20)		Total
	Freq	%	Freq	%	Freq	%	
Never			2	10.5	2	5.0	2
Sometimes	4	21.1	4	21.1	6	30.0	14
Always	15	78.9	13	68.4	14	70.0	42
Total	19	100.0	19	100.0	20	100.0	58
Pearson Chi-Square=4.71 p<.31							

Table 7-3

**The social worker should act as liaison between doctor and patient.
Frequencies and Percentages**

Responses	Municipal social worker (N=19)		Municipal doctor (N=19)		Municipal nurse (N=20)		Total
	Freq	%	Freq	%	Freq	%	
Never			1	5.0	2	10.0	3
Sometimes	3	15.8	5	25.0	4	20.0	12
Always	16	84.2	14	70.0	14	70.0	44
Total	19	100.0	20	100.0	20	100.0	59
Pearson Chi-Square=2.67 p<.28							

8. The eighth item analyzed in the survey was the degree to which social worker, doctors, and nurses from both settings agreed that the social worker should collaborate with other professionals on plan for patients care. Table 8-1 shows this analysis.

Table 8-1

**The social worker should collaborate with other professionals on plan for patients' care.
Frequencies and Percentages**

Responses	Municipal social worker (N=19)		Municipal doctor (N=19)		Municipal nurse (N=20)		Total
	Freq	%	Freq	%	Freq	%	
Never					2	5.0	4
Sometimes	2	5.3	8	20.5	6	15.0	16
Always	36	94.7	29	74.4	32	80.0	97
Total	38	100.0	39	100.0	40	100.0	117
Pearson Chi-Square=6.30 p<. 17							

All social workers (N=38, 100.0%), nearly all doctors (N=37) and nearly all nurses (N=38) agreed that the social worker should collaborate with other professionals on plan for patients' care. Only a small number of doctors (N=2) and nurses (N=2) agreed that the social worker should never collaborate with other professionals on plan for patients' care.

The difference in the perception of the role of the social worker in collaborating with other professionals on the plan for patients' care among social workers, doctors, and nurses was not statistically significant and the Null Hypothesis was accepted. Therefore, the hypothesis that social workers perceive theirs roles as providing both concrete and clinical services was not supported.

When the data was divided into two categories, municipal and voluntary, the result shows that all social workers from municipal hospitals (N=19) and all social workers from voluntary hospitals (N=19) agreed that the social worker should collaborate with other professionals on plan for patients' care. Nearly all doctors from municipal hospitals (N=17) and all doctors from voluntary hospitals (N=20) agreed that the social worker should collaborate with other professionals on plan for patients' care. Nearly all nurses from municipal hospitals (N=19) and nearly all nurses from voluntary hospitals (N=19) also agreed that the social worker should collaborate with other professional on plan for patients' care.

The difference in opinions about collaborating with other professionals on plan for patients' care among social workers, doctors, and nurses was not statistically significant in both settings and the Null Hypothesis was accepted. Therefore, the hypothesis that there will be no significant differences among doctors and nurses in their perception of the role of the social worker in the emergency room in both types of hospitals (municipal and voluntary) was not supported. See tables 8-2, 8-3.

Table 8-2

The social worker should collaborate with other professionals on plan for patients' care.
Frequencies and Percentages

Responses	Municipal social worker (N=19)		Municipal doctor (N=19)		Municipal nurse (N=20)		Total
	Freq	%	Freq	%	Freq	%	
Never			2	10.5	1	5.0	3
Sometimes	1	53.	2	10.5	3	15.0	6
Always	18	94.7	15	78.9	16	80.0	49
Total	19	100.0	19	100.0	20	100.0	58
Pearson Chi-Square=3.28 p<.51							

Table 8-3

The social worker should collaborate with other professionals on plan for patients' care.
Frequencies and Percentages

Responses	Municipal social worker (N=19)		Municipal doctor (N=19)		Municipal nurse (N=20)		Total
	Freq	%	Freq	%	Freq	%	
Never					1	5.0	
Sometimes	1	5.3	6	30.0	3	15.0	10
Always	18	94.7	14	70.0	16	80.0	48
Total	19	100.0	20	100.0	20	100.0	59
Pearson Chi-Square=6.27 p<.18							

9. The ninth item analyzed in the survey was the degree to which social workers, doctor, and nurses from both settings agree that the social worker should diagnose social problems of patients. Table 9-l shows this analysis.

Table 9-1

**The social worker should diagnose social problems of patients.
Frequencies and Percentages**

Responses	Municipal social worker (N=19)		Municipal doctor (N=19)		Municipal nurse (N=20)		Total
	Freq	%	Freq	%	Freq	%	
Sometimes	3	7.9	3	7.7	8	20.0	14
Always	35	92.1	36	92.3	32	80.0	103
Total	38	100.0	39	100.0	40	100.0	117
Pearson Chi-Square=3.72 p<.15							

All social workers (N=38), all doctors (N=39), and all nurses (N=40) agreed that the social worker should diagnose social problems of patients.

The difference in the perception of the role of the social worker in diagnosing social problems of patients was not statistically significant among social workers, doctors, and nurses and the Null Hypothesis was accepted. Therefore, the hypothesis that social workers perceive their roles as providing both concrete and clinical services was not supported.

When the data was divided into two categories, municipal and voluntary, the result shows that all social workers from municipal hospitals (N=19) and all social workers from voluntary hospitals (N=19) agreed that the social worker should diagnose social problems of patients. All doctors from municipal hospitals (N=20) and all doctors from voluntary hospitals (N=19) agreed that the social worker should diagnose social problems of patients. All nurses from voluntary hospitals (N=20) and all nurses from voluntary hospitals (N=20) agreed that the social worker should diagnose social problems of patients.

The difference in opinions about diagnosing social problems of patients among social workers, doctors, and nurses was statistically significant in municipal hospitals only and the Null Hypothesis was not accepted. Therefore, the hypothesis that there will be no significant differences among doctors and nurses in their perception of the role of the social worker in the emergency room in both types of hospitals (municipal and voluntary) was not supported. See tables 9-2, 9-3.

Table 9-2

The social worker should diagnose social problems of patients. Frequencies and Percentages

Responses	Municipal social worker (N=19)		Municipal doctor (N=19)		Municipal nurse (N=20)		Total
	Freq	%	Freq	%	Freq	%	
Sometimes					4	20.0	4
Always	19	100.0	19	100.0	16	80.0	54
Total	19	100.0	19	100.0	20	100.0	58
Pearson Chi-Square=8.16 p<.01							

TABLE 9-3

The social worker should diagnose social problems of patients, frequencies and percentages

Responses	Municipal social worker (N=19)		Municipal doctor (N=19)		Municipal nurse (N=20)		Total
	Freq	%	Freq	%	Freq	%	
Sometimes	3	15.8	3	15.0	4	20.0	10
Always	16	84.2	17	85.0	16	80.0	49
Total	19	100.0	20	100.0	20	100.0	59
Pearson Chi-Square=.20 p<.90							

10. The tenth item analyzed in the survey was the degree to which the social workers, doctors, and nurses from both settings

agreed that the social worker should determine patients' need for social services. Table 10-1 shows this analysis.

Table 10-1

The social worker should determine patients' need for social services. Frequencies and Percentages

Responses	Municipal social worker (N=19)		Municipal doctor (N=19)		Municipal nurse (N=20)		Total
	Freq	%	Freq	%	Freq	%	
Never					2	5.0	2
Sometimes	2	5.3	2	5.1	2	5.0	6
Always	36	94.7	37	94.9	36	90.0	109
Total	38	100.0	39	100.0	40	100.0	117
Pearson Chi-Square=3.91 p<.41							

All social workers (N=38), all doctors (N=39), and nearly all nurses (N=38) agreed that the social worker should determine patients' need for social services.

The difference in the perception of the role of the social worker in determining patients' need for social services among social workers, doctors, and nurses was not statistically significant and the Null Hypothesis was accepted. Therefore, the hypothesis that social workers perceive their role as providing both concrete and clinical services was not supported.

When the data was divided into two categories, municipal and voluntary, the result shows that all social workers from municipal hospitals (N=19) and all social workers from voluntary hospitals (N=19) agreed that the social worker should determine patients' need for social services. All doctors from municipal hospitals (N=19) and all doctors from voluntary hospitals (N=20) agreed that the social worker should determine patients' need for social services. Nearly all nurses from municipal hospitals (N=18) and nearly all nurses from voluntary hospitals (N=18) were also in agreement that the social worker should determine patients' need for social services. Only a small portion of social workers from municipal hospitals (N=1) and nurses from municipal hospitals (N=2) and nurses from voluntary hospitals (N=2) agreed that the social worker should never determine patients' need for social services.

The difference in opinions about determining patients' need for social services among social workers, doctors, and nurses was not statistically significant in both settings and the Null Hypothesis was accepted. Therefore, the hypothesis that there will be no signif-icant differences among doctors and nurses in their perception of the role of the social worker in the emergency room in both types of hospitals (municipal and voluntary) was not supported. See tables 10-1, 10-2.

Table 10-2

The social worker should determine patients' need for social services. Frequencies and Percentages

Responses	Municipal social worker (N=19)		Municipal doctor (N=19)		Municipal nurse (N=20)		Total
	Freq	%	Freq	%	Freq	%	
Sometimes	1	5.3			2	10.0	3
Always	18	94.7	19	100.0	18	90.0	55
Total	19	100.0	20	100.0			58
Pearson Chi-Square=1.98 p<.37							

Table 10-3

The social worker should determine patients' need for social services.
Frequencies and Percentages

Responses	Municipal social worker (N=19)		Municipal doctor (N=19)		Municipal nurse (N=20)		Total
	Freq	%	Freq	%	Freq	%	
Never					2	10.0	2
Sometimes		5.3	2	66.7			3
Always	18	94.7	18	90.0	18	90.0	54
Total	19	100.0	20	100.0	20	100.0	59
Pearson Chi-Square=1.98 p<.20							

11. The eleventh item analyzed in the survey was the degree to which social workers, doctors, and nurses from both settings agreed that the social worker should recommend treatment for mentally ill patients. Table 11-1 shows this analysis.

Table 11-1

The social worker should recommend treatment for mentally ill patients.
Frequencies and Percentages

Responses	Municipal social worker (N=19)		Municipal doctor (N=19)		Municipal nurse (N=20)		Total
	Freq	%	Freq	%	Freq	%	
Never	4	10.5	8	20.5	10	25.0	22
Sometimes	19	50.0	13	33.3	10	25.0	42
Always	15	39.5	18	46.2	20	50.0	53
Total	38	100.0	39	100.0	40	100.0	117
Pearson Chi-Square=6.24 p<.18							

The majority of social workers (N=34), doctors (N=33), and nurses (N=30) agreed that the social worker should recommend treatment for mentally ill patients. However, a significant number of nurses (N=10), doctors (N=8) than social workers (N=4) agreed that the social worker should never recommend treatment for mentally ill patients.

The difference in the perception of the role of the social worker in recommending treatment for mentally ill patients among social workers, doctors, and nurses was not statistically significant and the Null Hypothesis was accepted. Therefore, the hypothesis that social workers perceive their role as providing both concrete and clinical services was not supported.

When the data was divided into two categories, municipal and voluntary, the result shows that more social workers from municipal hospitals (N=18) than social workers from voluntary hospitals (N=16) agreed that the social worker should recommend treatment for mentally ill patients. About the same proportion of doctors from municipal hospitals (N=15) and doctors from voluntary hospitals (N=16) agreed that the social worker should recommend treatment for mentally ill patients. More nurses from municipal hospitals (N=17) than nurses from voluntary hospitals (N=13) agreed that the social worker should recommend treatment for mentally ill patients.

The difference in opinions about recommending treatment for mentally ill patients among social workers, doctors, and nurses was statistically significant in voluntary hospitals and the Null Hypothesis was rejected. Therefore, the hypothesis that there will be no significant differences among doctors and nurses in their perceptions of the role of the social worker in the emergency room in both types of hospitals (municipal and voluntary) was supported. See tables 11-2. 11-3.

Table 11-2

The social worker should recommend treatment for mentally ill patients.
Frequencies and Percentages

Responses	Municipal social worker (N=19)		Municipal doctor (N=19)		Municipal nurse (N=20)		Total
	Freq	%	Freq	%	Freq	%	
Never	1	5.3	4	21.1	3	15.0	8
Sometimes	7	36.8	7	36.8	7	35.0	21
Always	11	57.9	8	42.1	10	50.0	29
Total	19	100.0	19	100.0	20	100.0	58
Pearson Chi-Square=2.23 p<.69							

Table 11-3

The social worker should recommend treatment for mentally ill patients.
Frequencies and Percentages

Responses	Municipal social worker (N=19)		Municipal doctor (N=19)		Municipal nurse (N=20)		Total
	Freq	%	Freq	%	Freq	%	
Never	3					35.0	14
Sometimes	12	63.2	6	30.0	3	15.0	21
Always	4	21.1	10	50.0	10	50.0	24
Total	19	100.0	20	100.0	20	100.0	59
Pearson Chi-Square=10.9 p<.02							

12. The twelfth item analyzed in the survey was the degree to which the social worker, doctors, and nurses from both settings agreed that the social worker should strengthen patients' participation in their own care. Table 12-1 shows this analysis.

Table 12-1

The social worker should strengthen patients' participation in their own care.
Frequencies and Percentages.

Responses	Municipal social worker (N=19)		Municipal doctor (N=19)		Municipal nurse (N=20)		Total
	Freq	%	Freq	%	Freq	%	
Sometimes	8	21.1	9	23.1	8	20.0	25
Always	30	78.9	29	74.4	29	72.5	88
Total	38	100.0	39	100.0	40	100.0	117
Pearson Chi-Square=3.53 p<.47							

All social workers (N=38). nearly all doctors (N=38), and nearly all nurses (N=37) agreed that the social worker should strengthen patients' participation in their own care. However, a small proportion of doctors (N=1) and nurses (N=3) disagreed.

The difference in the perception of the role of the social worker in strengthening patients' participation in their own care among social workers, doctors, and nurses was not statistically significant and the Null Hypothesis was accepted. Therefore, the hypothesis that doctors and nurses are more likely to perceive the role of the social worker in the emergency room as providing concrete rather than clinical services was not supported.

When the data was divided into two categories, municipal and voluntary, the result shows that all social workers from municipal hospitals (N=19) and nearly all social workers from voluntary hospitals (N=19) agreed that the social worker should strengthen patients' participation in their own care. A small proportion of social workers (N=3) from municipal hospitals disagree. All doctors from municipal hospitals (N=19) and nearly all doctors from voluntary hospitals (N=19) agreed that the social worker should strengthen patients' participation in their own care. All nurses from municipal hospitals (N=20) and most nurses from voluntary hospitals (N=17) agreed that the social worker should strengthen patients' participation in their own care.

The difference in opinions about strengthening patients' participation in their own care among social workers, doctors, and nurses was not statistically significant and the Null Hypothesis was accepted. Therefore, the hypothesis that there will be no significant differences among doctors and nurses in their perceptions of the role of the social worker in the emergency room in both types of hospitals (municipal and voluntary) was not supported. See tables 12-2, 12-3.

Table 12-2
The social worker should strengthen patients' participation in their own care.
Frequencies and Percentages

Responses	Municipal social worker (N=19)		Municipal doctor (N=19)		Municipal nurse (N=20)		Total
	Freq	%	Freq	%	Freq	%	
Sometimes	3	15.8	5	26.3	4	20.0	12
Always	16	84.2	14	73.7	16	80.0	46
Total	19	100.0	19	100.0	20	100.0	58
Pearson Chi-Square=.65 p<.72							

Table 12-3

The social worker should strengthen patients' participation in their own care.
Frequencies and Percentages

Responses	Municipal social worker (N=19)		Municipal doctor (N=19)		Municipal nurse (N=20)		Total
	Freq	%	Freq	%	Freq	%	
Never			1	5.0	3	15.0	4
Sometimes	5	26.3	4	20.0	4	20.0	13
Always	14	73.7	15	75.0	13	65.0	42
Total	19	100.0	20	100.0	20	100.0	59
Pearson Chi-Square=3.77 p<.43							

13. The thirteenth item analyzed in the survey was the degree to which the social workers, doctors, and nurses from both settings agreed that the social worker should help patients overcome personal crisis. Table 13-1 shows this analysis.

Table 13-1

The social worker should help patients overcome personal crisis.
Frequencies and Percentages

Responses	Municipal social worker (N=19)		Municipal doctor (N=19)		Municipal nurse (N=20)		Total
	Freq	%	Freq	%	Freq	%	
Never			1	2.6	1	2.5	2
Sometimes	7	18.4	4	10.3	10	25.0	21
Always	31	81.6	34	87.2	29	72.5	94
Total	38	100.0	39	100.0	40	100.0	117
Pearson chi-Square=3.90 p=<.42							

All social workers (N=38), Nearly all doctors (N=38), and nearly all nurses (N=39) agreed that the social worker should help patients overcome personal crisis.

The difference in the perception of the role of the social worker in helping patients overcome personal crisis among social workers, doctors, and nurses was not statistically significant and the Null Hypothesis was accepted. Therefore, the hypothesis that social workers perceive their role as providing both concrete and clinical services was not supported.

When the data was divided into two categories, municipal and voluntary, the result from this analysis shows that all social workers from municipal hospitals (N=19) and all social workers from voluntary hospitals (N=19) agreed that the social worker should help patients overcome personal crises. All doctors from municipal hospitals (N= 19) and nearly all doctors from voluntary hospitals (N=19) agreed that the social worker should help patients overcome personal crisis. A small proportion of doctors from municipal hospitals (N=2) and doctors from voluntary hospitals (N=1) disagreed. All nurses from municipal hospitals (N=20) and nearly all nurses from voluntary hospitals (N=19) agreed that the social worker should help patients overcome personal cns1s. Only a small proportion of nurses from voluntary hospitals (N=1) disagreed.

The difference in opinions about helping patients overcome personal crisis among social workers, doctors, and nurses was not statistically significant in both hospitals and the Null Hypothesis was accepted. Therefore, the hypothesis that there will be no significant differences among doctors and nurses in their perceptions of the role of the social worker in the emergency room in both types of hospitals (municipal and voluntary) was not supported. See tables 13-2, 13-3.

Table 13-2

The social worker should help patients overcome personal crisis. Frequencies and Percentages

Responses	Municipal social worker (N=19)		Municipal doctor (N=19)		Municipal nurse (N=20)		Total
	Freq	%	Freq	%	Freq	%	
Sometimes	3	15.8	2	10.5	6	30.0	12
Always	16	84.2	17	89.5	14	70.0	46
Total	19	100.0	19	100.0	20	100.0	58
Pearson Chi-Square=2.59 p<.27							

Table 13-3

The social worker should help patients overcome personal crisis. Frequencies and percentages

Responses	Municipal social worker (N=19)		Municipal doctor (N=19)		Municipal nurse (N=20)		Total
	Freq	%	Freq	%	Freq	%	
Never			1	5.0	1	5.0	3
Sometimes	4	21.1	2	10.0	4	20.0	10
Always	15	78.9	17	85.0	15	75.0	47
Total	19	100.0	20	100.0	20	100.0	59
Pearson Chi-Square=1.94 p<.74							

14. The fourteenth item analyzed in the survey was the degree to which the social workers, doctors, and nurses from both settings agreed that the social worker should encourage patients to follow medical advise. Table 14-1 shows this analysis.

Table 14-1

The social worker should encourage patients to follow medical recommendations.
Frequencies and Percentages

Responses	Municipal social worker (N=19)		Municipal doctor (N=19)		Municipal nurse (N=20)		Total
	Freq	%	Freq	%	Freq	%	
Never					1	2.5	1
Sometimes	8	21.1	7	10	17.9	10	25
Always	30	78.9	32	82.1	29	72.5	91
Total	38	100.0	39	100.0	40	100.0	117
Pearson Chi-Square=2.62 p<.62							

All social workers (N=38), doctors (N=39), and nearly all nurses (N=39) agreed that the social worker should encourage patients to follow medical recommendations.

Only a small proportion of nurses (N=1) disagreed. The difference in the perception of the role of the social worker in encouraging patients to follow medical recommendations among social workers, doctors, and nurses was not statistically significant and the Null Hypothesis was accepted. Therefore, the hypothesis that doctors and nurses are more likely to perceive the role of the social worker in the emergency room as providing concrete rather than clinical services was not supported.

When the data was divided into two categories, municipal and voluntary, the result from this analysis shows that all social workers from municipal hospitals (N=19) and all social workers from voluntary hospitals (N=19) agreed that the social worker should encourage patients to follow medical recommendations. All doctors from municipal hospitals (N=19) and all doctors from voluntary hospitals (N=20) agreed that the social worker should encourage patients to follow medical recommendations. All nurses from municipal hospitals (N=20) and nearly all nurses from voluntary hospitals (N=19) agreed that the social worker should encourage patients to follow medical recommendations. Only a small proportion of nurses from municipal hospitals (N=1) disagreed.

The difference in opinion about encouraging patients to follow medical recommendations among social workers, doctors, and nurses was not statistically significant in both settings and the Null Hypothesis was accepted. Therefore, the hypothesis that there will be no significant differences among doctors and nurses in their perception of the role of the social worker in both types of hospitals (municipal and voluntary) was not supported. See tables 14-2, 14-3.

Table 14-2

The social worker should encourage patients to follow medical recommendations.
Frequencies and Percentages

Responses	Municipal social worker (N=19)		Municipal doctor (N=19)		Municipal nurse (N=20)		Total
	Freq	%	Freq	%	Freq	%	
Sometimes	4	21.1	3	15.8	4	20.0	11
Always	15	78.9	16	84.2	16	80.0	47
Total	19	100.0	19	100.0	20	100.0	58
Pearson Chi-Square=.19 p<.90							

Table 14-3

The social worker should encourage patients to follow medical recommendations.
Frequencies and Percentages

Responses	Municipal social worker (N=19)		Municipal doctor (N=19)		Municipal nurse (N=20)		Total
	Freq	%	Freq	%	Freq	%	
Never					1	5.0	1
Sometimes	4	21.1	4	20.0	6	30.0	14
Always	15	78.9	16	80.0	13	65.0	44
Total	19	100.0	20	100.0	20	100.0	59
Pearson Chi-Square=2.83 p<.58							

15. The fifteenth item analyzed in the survey was the degree to which social workers, doctors, and nurses from both settings agreed that the social worker should provide emotional support to patients. Table 15-1 shows this analysis.

Table 15-1

The social worker should provide emotional support to patients.
Frequencies and Percentages

Responses	Municipal social worker (N=19)		Municipal doctor (N=19)		Municipal nurse (N=20)		Total
	Freq	%	Freq	%	Freq	%	
Never		3	7.7	1	2.5	4	
Sometimes	1	2.6	5	12.8	8	20.0	14
Always	37	97.4	31	79.5	31	77.5	99
Total	38	100.0	39	100.0	40	100.0	117
Pearson Chi-Square=9.52 p<. 04							

All social workers (N=38), nearly all doctors (N=36), and nearly all nurses (N=39) agreed that the social worker should provide emotional support to patients.

The difference in the perception of the role of the social worker in providing emotional support to patients among social workers, doctors, and nurses was statistically significant and the Null Hypothesis was rejected. Therefore, the hypothesis that social workers perceive their role as providing both concrete and clinical services was supported. When the data was divided into two categories, municipal and voluntary, the result from this analysis shows that all social workers from municipal hospitals (N=19) and all social workers from voluntary hospitals (N=19) agreed that the social worker should provide emotional support to patients. Nearly all doctors from municipal hospitals (N=17) and nearly all doctors from voluntary hospitals (N=19) agreed that the social worker should provide emotional support to patients. All nurses from municipal hospitals (N=20) and nearly all nurses from voluntary hospitals (N=19) agreed that the social worker should provide emotional support to patients.

The difference in opinions about providing emotional support to patients among social workers, doctors, and social workers was statistically significant in municipal hospitals only and the Null Hypothesis was accepted. Therefore, the hypothesis that there will be no significant differences among doctors and nurses in their perception of the role of the social worker in the emergency room in both types of hospitals (municipal and voluntary) was not supported. See tables 15-2, 15-3.

Table 15-2

**The social worker should provide emotional support to patients.
Frequencies and Percentages**

Responses	Municipal social worker (N=19)		Municipal doctor (N=19)		Municipal nurse (N=20)		Total
	Freq	%	Freq	%	Freq	%	
Never			2	10.5			2
Sometimes			1	5.3	5	20.5	6
Always	19	100.0	16	84.2	15	75.0	50
Total	19	100.0	19	100.0	20	100.0	58
Pearson Chi-Square= 11.41 p<. 02							

Table 15-3

**The social worker should provide emotional support to patients.
Frequencies and Percentages**

Responses	Municipal social worker (N=19)		Municipal doctor (N=19)		Municipal nurse (N=20)		Total
	Freq	%	Freq	%	Freq	%	
Never			1	5.0	1	5.0	2
Sometimes	1	5.3	4	20.0	3	15.0	8
Always	18	94.7	15	75.0	16	80.0	49
Total	19	100.0	20	100.0	20	100.0	58
Pearson Chi-Square=3.04 p<.55							

16. The sixteenth item analyzed in the survey was the degree to which the social workers, doctors, and nurses from both settings agreed that the social worker should help patients adjust to illness. Table 16-1 shows this analysis.

Table 16-1

The social worker should help patients adjust to illness. Frequencies and Percentages

Responses	Municipal social worker (N=19)		Municipal doctor (N=19)		Municipal nurse (N=20)		Total
	Freq	%	Freq	%	Freq	%	
Never			2	5.1	2	5.0	4
Sometimes	6	15.8	14	35.9	16	40.0	36
Always	32	84.2	23	59.0	22	55.0	77
Total	38	100.0	39	100.0	40	100.0	117
Pearson Chi-Square=9.07 p<.05							

The result from this analysis shows that all social workers (N=38) nearly all doctors (N=37) and nearly all nurses (N=38) agreed that the social worker should help patients adjust to illness.

The difference in the perception of the role of the social worker in the emergency room among social workers, doctors, and nurses was statistically significant and the Null hypothesis was rejected. Therefore, the hypothesis that social workers perceive their role as providing both concrete and clinical services was supported.

When the data was divided into two categories, municipal and voluntary, the result from this analysis shows that all social workers from municipal hospitals (N=19) and all social workers from voluntary hospitals (N=19) agreed that the social worker should help patients adjust to illness. Nearly all doctors from municipal hospitals (N=18) and nearly all doctors from voluntary hospitals (N=19) agreed that the social worker should help patients adjust to illness. All nurses from municipal hospitals (N=20) and nearly all nurses from voluntary hospitals (N=18) agreed that the social worker should help patients adjust to illness.

The difference in opinions about helping patients adjust to illness among social workers, doctors, and nurses was not statistically significant in both settings and the Null hypothesis was accepted.

Therefore, the hypothesis that there will be no significant differences among doctors and nurses in their perception of the role of the social worker in the emergency room by types of hospitals (municipal and voluntary) was not supported. See tables 16-2, 16-3.

17. The seventeenth item analyzed in the survey was the degree to which social workers, doctors, and nurses from both settings agreed that the social worker should provide psychotherapy to emotionally disturbed patients. Table 17-1 shows this analysis.

Table 17-1

The social worker should provide psychotherapy to emotionally disturbed patients.
Frequencies and Percentages

Responses	Municipal social worker (N=19)		Municipal doctor (N=19)		Municipal nurse (N=20)		Total
	Freq	%	Freq	%	Freq	%	
Never	5	13.2	8	20.5	10	25.0	23
Sometimes	11	28.9	16	41.0	14	35.0	41
Always	22	57.9	15	38.5	16	40.0	53
Total	38	100.0	39	100.0	40	100.0	117
Pearson Chi-Square=4.9 p<.38							

The result from this analysis shows that most social workers (N=33, 86.8%), doctors (N=31), and nurses (N=30) agreed that the social worker should provide psychotherapy to emotionally disturbed patients. However, a larger proportion of nurses (N=10) and doctors (N=8) than social workers (N=5) disagreed.

The difference in the perception of the role of the social worker in providing psychotherapy to emotionally disturbed patients among social workers, doctors, and nurses was not statistically significant and the Null hypothesis was accepted. Therefore, the hypothesis that doctors and nurses are more likely to perceive the role of the social worker in the emergency room as providing concrete rather than clinical services was not supported.

When the data was divided into two categories, municipal and voluntary, the result show that more social workers from municipal hospitals (N=18) than social workers from voluntary hospitals (N=15) agreed that the social worker should provide psychotherapy to emotionally disturbed patients. More doctors from voluntary hospitals (N=17) than doctors from municipal hospitals (N=14) agreed that the social worker should provide psychotherapy to emotionally disturbed patients. More nurses from voluntary hospitals (N=16) than nurses from municipal hospitals (N=14) agreed that the social worker should provide psychotherapy to emotionally disturbed patients.

The difference in opinions about providing psychotherapy to emotionally disturbed patients among social workers, doctors, and nurses was not statistically significant in both settings and the Null hypothesis was accepted. Therefore, the hypothesis that there will be no significant differences among doctors and nurses in their perception of the role of the social worker in the emergency room in both types of hospitals (municipal and voluntary) was not supported. See tables 17-2. 173.

Table 17-2

The social worker should provide psychotherapy to emotionally disturbed patients.
Frequencies and Percentages

Responses	Municipal social worker (N=19)		Municipal doctor (N=19)		Municipal nurse (N=20)		Total
	Freq	%	Freq	%	Freq	%	
Never	1	5.3	5	26.4	6	30.0	12
Sometimes	6	31.6	7	36.8	5	25.0	18
Always	12	63.1	7	36.8	9	45.0	28
Total	19	100.0	19	100.0	20	100.0	58
Pearson Chi-Square=5.18 p<.26							

Table 17-3

The social worker should provide psychotherapy to emotionally disturbed patients.
Frequencies and Percentages

Responses	Municipal social worker (N=19)		Municipal doctor (N=19)		Municipal nurse (N=20)		Total
	Freq	%	Freq	%	Freq	%	
Never	4	21.1	3	15.0	4	20.0	11
Sometimes	5	26.3	9	45.0	9	45.0	23
Always	10	52.6	8	40.0	7	35.0	25
Total	19	100.0	20	100.0	20	100.0	59
Pearson Chi-Square=2.13 p<.71							

18. The eighteenth item analyzed in the survey was the degree to which social workers, doctors, and nurses from both settings agreed that the social worker should use psychotherapeutic techniques with patients. Table 18-1 shows this analysis.

Table 18-1

The social worker should use psychotherapeutic techniques with patients.
Frequencies and Percentages

Responses	Municipal social worker (N=19)		Municipal doctor (N=19)		Municipal nurse (N=20)		Total
	Freq	%	Freq	%	Freq	%	
Never	3	7.9	8	20.5	9	22.5	20
Sometimes	13	34.2	16	41.0	14	35.0	43
Always	22	57.9	15	38.5	17	42.5	54
Total	38	100.0	39	100.0	40	100.0	117
Pearson Chi-Square=4.87 p<.30							

The result from this analysis shows that most social workers (N=35), doctors (N=31), and nurses (N=31) agreed that the social worker should use psychotherapeutic techniques with patients. However, a larger proportion of nurses (N=9) and doctors (N=8) than social workers (N=3) disagreed.

The difference in the perception of the role of the social worker in using psychotherapeutic techniques with patients among social workers, doctors, and nurses was not statistically significant and the Null hypothesis was accepted. Therefore, the hypothesis that doctors and nurses are more likely to perceive the role of the social worker in the emergency room as providing concrete rather than clinical services was not supported.

When the data was divided into two categories, municipal and voluntary, the data shows that nearly all social workers from municipal hospitals (N=18) and social workers from voluntary hospitals (N=17) agreed that the social worker should use psychotherapeutic techniques with patients. About the same proportion of doctors from municipal hospitals (N=17) and doctors from voluntary hospitals (N=14) agreed that the social worker should use psychotherapeutic techniques with patients. More nurses from voluntary hospitals (N=17) than nurses from municipal hospitals (N=14) agreed that the social worker should use psychotherapeutic techniques with patients.

The difference in opinions about using psychotherapeutic techniques with patients among social workers, doctors, and nurses was not statistically significant in both settings and the Null hypothesis was accepted. Therefore, the hypothesis that there will be no significant differences between doctors and nurses in their perception of the role of the social worker in the emergency room in both hospital settings (municipal and voluntary) was not supported. See tables 18-2, 18-3.

Table 18-2

The social worker should provide psychotherapeutic techniques with patients.
Frequencies and Percentages

Responses	Municipal social worker (N=19)		Municipal doctor (N=19)		Municipal nurse (N=20)		Total
	Freq	%	Freq	%	Freq	%	
Never	1	5.3	5	26.3	6	30.0	12
Sometimes	6	31.6	5	26.3	5	25.0	16
Always	12	63.2	9	47.4	9	45.0	30
Total	19	100.0	19	100.0	20	100.0	58
Pearson Chi-Square=4.20 p<.37							

Table 18-3

The social worker should provide psychotherapeutic techniques with patients.
Frequencies and Percentages

Responses	Municipal social worker (N=19)		Municipal doctor (N=19)		Municipal nurse (N=20)		Total
	Freq	%	Freq	%	Freq	%	
Never	7	10.5	3	15.0	3	15.0	8
Sometimes	7	36.8	11	55.0	9	45.0	27
Always	10	52.6	6	30.0	8	40.0	24
Total	19	100.0	20	100.0	20	100.0	59
Pearson Chi-Square=2.19 p.71							

19. The nineteenth item in the survey analyzed was the degree to which social workers, doctors, and nurses from both settings agreed that the social worker should provide post-hospital employment counseling to patients. Table 19-1 shows this analysis.

Table 19-1

The social worker should provide post-hospital employment counseling to patients.
Frequencies and Percentages

Responses	Municipal social worker (N=19)		Municipal doctor (N=19)		Municipal nurse (N=20)		Total
	Freq	%	Freq	%	Freq	%	
Never	12	31.6	5	12.8	5	12.5	22
Sometimes	19	50.0	14	35.9	12	30.0	45
Always	7	18.4	20	51.3	23	57.5	50
Total	38	100.0	39	100.0	40	100.0	117
Pearson Chi-Square=14.97 p<.01							

The result from this analysis shows that more nurses (N=35) and doctors (N=34) than social workers (N=16) agreed that the social worker should provide post-hospital employment counseling to patients. However, a significant larger number of social workers (N=12) compared to the number of doctors (N=5) and nurses (N=5) disagreed.

The difference in the perception of the role of the social worker in providing post hospital employment counseling to patients among social workers, doctors, and nurses was statistically significant and the Null hypothesis was rejected. Therefore. the hypothesis that doctors and nurses are more likely to perceive the role of the social worker in the emergency room as providing concrete rather than clinical services was supported.

When the data was divided into two categories, municipal and voluntary, the result shows that more social workers from municipal hospitals (N=14) than social workers from voluntary hospitals (N=11) agreed that the social worker should provide post-hospital employment counseling to patients. More doctors from municipal hospitals (N=18) than doctors from voluntary hospitals (N=16) agreed that the social worker should provide post-hospital employment counseling to patients. More nurses from municipal hospitals (N=18) than nurses from voluntary hospitals (N=17) agreed that the social worker should provide post-hospital employment to patients. A larger proportion of social workers from voluntary hospitals (N=8) than social workers from municipal hospitals (N=4) disagreed. More doctors from municipal hospitals (N=3) than doctors from voluntary hospitals (N=2) disagreed. More nurses from voluntary hospitals (N=3) than nurses from municipal hospitals (N=2) disagreed.

The difference in opinions about providing post-hospital employment counseling to patients among social workers, doctors, and nurses was statistically significant in voluntary hospitals only and the Null hypothesis was accepted. Therefore, the hypothesis that there will be no significant differences between doctors and nurses in their perception of the role of the social worker in the emergency room in both types of hospitals (municipal and voluntary) was not supported. See tables 19-2, 19-3.

Table 19-2

The social worker should provide post-hospital counseling to patients.
Frequencies and Percentages

Responses	Municipal social worker (N=19)		Municipal doctor (N=19)		Municipal nurse (N=20)		Total
	Freq	%	Freq	%	Freq	%	
Never	4	21.1	3	15.8	2	10.0	9
Sometimes	11	57.8	6	31.6	8	40.0	25
Always	4	21.1	10	52.6	10	50.0	24
Total	19	100.0	19	100.0	20	100.0	58
Pearson Chi-Square=5.20 p<.26							

Table 19-3

The social worker should provide post-hospital counseling to patients.
Frequencies and Percentages

Responses	Municipal social worker (N=19)		Municipal doctor (N=19)		Municipal nurse (N=20)		Total
	Freq	%	Freq	%	Freq	%	
Never	8	42.1	2	10.0	3	15.0	9
Sometimes	8	42.1	8	40.0	4	20.0	25
Always	3	15.8	10	50.0	13	65.0	26
Total	19	100.0	20	100.0	20	100.0	59
Pearson Chi-Square=12.5 p<.01							

20. The twentieth item in the survey analyzed was the degree to which social workers, doctors, and nurses from both settings agreed that the social worker should conduct pre-discharge study of homes. Table 20-1 shows this analysis.

Table 20-1

The social worker should conduct pre-discharge study of home.
Frequencies and Percentages

Responses	Municipal social worker (N=19)		Municipal doctor (N=19)		Municipal nurse (N=20)		Total
	Freq	%	Freq	%	Freq	%	
Never	14	36.8	4	10.3	3	7.5	21
Sometimes	11	28.9	13	33.3	14	35.0	38
Always	13	34.2	22	56.4	23	57.5	58
Total	38	100.0	39	100.0	40	100.0	117
Pearson Chi-Square=14.93 p<.01							

The result from this analysis shows that more nurses (N=37) and doctors (N=35) than social workers (N=24) agreed that the social worker should conduct pre-discharge study of homes.

The difference in the perception of the role of the social worker in conducting pre-discharge study of homes by social workers, doctors, and nurses was statistically significant and the Null hypothesis was rejected. Therefore, the hypothesis that doctors and nurses are more likely to perceive the role of the social worker in the emergency room as providing concrete rather than clinical services was supported.

When the data was divided into two categories, municipal and voluntary, the result shows that more social workers from municipal hospitals (N=14) than social workers from voluntary hospitals (N=10) agreed that the social worker should conduct pre-discharge study of homes. Nearly all doctors from municipal hospitals (N=18) and doctors from voluntary hospitals (N=17) agreed that the social worker should conduct pre-discharge study of homes. Nearly all nurses from municipal hospitals (N=18) and nearly all nurses from voluntary hospitals (N=17) agreed that the social worker should conduct pre- discharge study of homes.

The difference in opinion about conducting pre-discharge study of homes among social workers, doctors, and nurses was statistically significant in both settings and the Null hypothesis was rejected. Therefore, the hypothesis that there will be no significant differences between doctors and nurses in their perception of the role of the social worker in the emergency room in both types of hospitals (municipal and voluntary) was supported. See tables 20-2, 20-3

Table 20-2

The social worker should conduct pre-discharge study of homes. Frequencies and Percentages

Responses	Municipal social worker (N=19)		Municipal doctor (N=19)		Municipal nurse (N=20)		Total
	Freq	%	Freq	%	Freq	%	
Never	5	26.3	1	5.3	2	10.0	8
Sometimes	4	21.1	6	31.5	7	35.0	17
Always	10	52.6	12	63.2	11	55.0	33
Total	19	100.0	19	100.0	20	100.0	58

Pearson chi-Square=4.27 p<.04

Table 20-3

The social worker should conduct pre-discharge study of home. Frequencies and Percentages

Responses	Municipal social worker (N=19)		Municipal doctor (N=19)		Municipal nurse (N=20)		Total
	Freq	%	Freq	%	Freq	%	
Never	9	47.4	3	15.0	1	5.0	13
Sometimes	7	36.8	7	35.0	7	35.0	21
Always	3	15.8	10	50.0	12	60.0	25
Total	19	100.0	20	100.0	30	100.0	59

Pearson Chi-Square=13.4 p<.01

21. The twenty-first item in the survey analyzed was the degree to which social workers, doctors, and nurses from both settings agreed that the social worker should refer families to community agencies. Table 21-1 shows this analysis.

Table 21-1

The social worker should refer families to community agencies. Frequencies and Percentages

Responses	Municipal social worker (N=19)		Municipal doctor (N=19)		Municipal nurse (N=20)		Total
	Freq	%	Freq	%	Freq	%	
Sometimes	4	10.5	6	15.4	4	10.0	14
Always	34	89.5	33	84.6	36	90.0	103
Total	38	100.0	39	100.0	40	100.0	117
Pearson Chi-Square=65 p.<72							

The result from this analysis shows that all social workers (N=38), doctors, (N=39), and nurses (N=40) agreed that the social worker should refer families to community agencies.

The difference in the perception of the role of the social worker in referring families to community agencies among social workers, doctors, and nurses was not statistically significant and the Null hypothesis was accepted. Therefore, the hypothesis that doctors and nurses are more likely to perceive the role of the social worker in the emergency room as providing concrete rather than clinical services was not supported.

When the data was divided into two categories, municipal and voluntary, the result shows that more social workers from voluntary hospitals (N=19) than social workers from municipal hospitals (N=15) agreed that the social worker should refer families to community agencies. More doctors from municipal hospitals (N=18) than doctors from voluntary hospitals (N=15) agreed that the social worker should refer families to community agencies. Most nurses from municipal hospitals (N=19) and most nurses from voluntary hospitals (N=19) agreed that the social worker should refer families to community agencies.

The difference in opinions about referring families to community agencies among social workers, doctors, ad nurses was not statistically significant in both settings and the Null hypothesis was accepted. Therefore, the hypothesis that there will be no significant differences between doctors and nurses in their perception of the role of the social worker in the emergency room in both types of hospitals (municipal and voluntary) was not supported. See tables 21-2. 21-3.

Table 21-1

The social worker should refer families to community agencies. Frequencies and Percentages

Responses	Municipal social worker (N=19)		Municipal doctor (N=19)		Municipal nurse (N=20)		Total
	Freq	%	Freq	%	Freq	%	
Sometimes	4	21.1	1	5.3	1	5.0	6
Always	15	78.9	18	94.7	19	95.0	52
Total	19	100.0	19	100.0	20	100.0	58

Pearson Chi-Square=3.49 p<.17

Table 21-3

The social worker should refer families to community agencies. Frequencies and Percentages

Responses	Municipal social worker (N=19)		Municipal doctor (N=19)		Municipal nurse (N=20)		Total
	Freq	%	Freq	%	Freq	%	
Sometimes			5	25.0	1	5.0	6
Always	19	100.0	15	75.0	19	95.0	53
Total	19	100.0	20	100.0	20	100.0	59

Pearson Chi-Square=5.24 p<.07

22. The twenty-second item in the survey analyzed was the degree to which social workers, doctors, and nurses agreed that the social worker should interpret hospital services to community agencies. Table 22-1 shows this analysis.

Table 22-1

The social worker should interpret hospital services to community agencies.
Frequencies and Percentages

Responses	Municipal social worker (N=19)		Municipal doctor (N=19)		Municipal nurse (N=20)		Total
	Freq	%	Freq	%	Freq	%	
Never	2	5.3	3	7.7	2	5.0	7
Sometimes	19	50.0	6	15.4	9	22.5	34
Always	17	44.7	30	76.9	29	72.5	76
Total	38	100.0	39	100.0	40	100.0	117
Pearson Chi-Square= 12.72 p<.0l							

Nearly all social workers (N=35), doctors (N=36), and nurses (N=38) agreed that the social worker should interpret hospital services to community agencies. A small proportion of social workers (N=2), doctors (N=3) and nurses (N=2) disagreed.

The difference in the perception of the role of the social worker in the emergency room in interpreting hospital services to community agencies among social workers, doctors, and nurses was statistically significant and the Null hypothesis was rejected.

Therefore, the hypothesis that doctors and nurses are more likely to perceive the role of the social worker in the emergency room as providing concrete rather than clinical services was supported.

When the data was divided into two categories, municipal and voluntary, the result shows that all social workers from municipal hospitals (N=19) and nearly all social workers from voluntary hospitals (N=17) agreed that the social worker should interpret hospital services to community agencies. Nearly all doctors from municipal hospitals (N=18) and nearly all doctors from voluntary hospitals (N=18) agreed that the social worker should interpret hospital services to community agencies. Nearly all nurses from municipal hospitals (N=19) and nearly all nurses from voluntary hospitals (N=19) agreed that the social worker should interpret hospital services to community agencies.

The difference in opinions about interpreting hospital services to community agencies among social workers, doctors, and nurses was not statistically significant in both settings and the Null hypothesis was accepted. Therefore, the hypothesis that there will be no significant differences between doctors and nurses in their perceptions of the role of the social worker in the emergency room in both types of hospitals (municipal and voluntary) was not supported. See tables 22-2. 22-3.

Table 22-2

The social worker should interpret hospital services to community agencies.
Frequencies and Percentages

Responses	Municipal social worker (N=19)		Municipal doctor (N=19)		Municipal nurse (N=20)		Total
	Freq	%	Freq	%	Freq	%	
Never			1	5.3	1	5.0	2
Sometimes	9	47.4	2	10.5	3	15.0	14
Always	10	52.6	16	84.2	16	80.0	42
Total	19	100.0	19	100.0	20	100.0	58
Pearson Chi-Square=5.77 p<.21							

Table 22-3

The social worker should interpret hospital services to community agencies.
Frequencies and Percentages

Responses	Municipal social worker (N=19)		Municipal doctor (N=19)		Municipal nurse (N=20)		Total
	Freq	%	Freq	%	Freq	%	
Never	2	10.6	2	10.0	1	5.0	5
Sometimes	10	52.6	4	20.0	6	30.0	20
Always	7	36.8	14	70.0	13	65.0	34
Total	19	100.0	20	100.0	20	100.0	59
Pearson Chi-Squares.92 p<.22							

23. The twenty-third item in the survey analyzed was the degree to which social workers, doctors, and nurses from both settings agreed that the social worker should organize ex-patient groups to improve hospital resources. Table 23-1 shows this analysis.

Table 23-1

The social worker should organize ex-patient groups to improve hospital resources.
Frequencies and Percentages

Responses	Municipal social worker (N=19)		Municipal doctor (N=19)		Municipal nurse (N=20)		Total
	Freq	%	Freq	%	Freq	%	
Never	5	13.2	16	41.1	4	10.0	25
Sometimes	9	23.7	20	51.2	18	45.0	47
Always	24	63.1	3	7.7	18	45.0	45
Total	38	100.0	39	100.0	40	100.0	117
Pearson Chi-Square=30.7 p<.01							

Moore nurses (N=36) and social workers (N=33) than doctors (N=23) agreed that the social worker should organize ex-patient groups to improve hospital resources.

The difference in the perception of the role of the social worker in organizing ex-patient groups to improve hospital resources among social workers, doctors, and nurses was statistically significant and the Null hypothesis was rejected. Therefore, the hypothesis that doctors and nurses are more likely to perceive the role of the social worker in the emergency room as providing concrete rather than clinical services was supported.

When the data was divided into two categories, municipal and voluntary, the result shows that more social workers from municipal hospitals (N=12) than social workers from voluntary hospitals (N=10) agreed that the social worker should organize ex-patient groups to improve hospital resources. An equal number of doctors from municipal hospitals (N=17) and doctors from voluntary hospitals (N=17) agreed that the social worker should organize ex-patient groups to improve hospital resources. Nearly all nurses from municipal hospitals (N=17) and nearly all nurses from voluntary hospitals (N=19) agreed that the social worker should organize ex- patient groups to improve hospitals resources.

The difference in opinions about organizing ex-patient groups to improve hospital resources among social workers, doctors, and nurses was statistically significant in both settings and the Null hypothesis was rejected. Therefore, the hypothesis that there will be no differences among doctors and nurses in their perception of the role of the social worker in the emergency room by types of hospitals (municipal and voluntary) was supported. See tables 23-2, 23-3.

Table 23-2

The social worker should organize ex-patient groups to improve hospital resources.
Frequencies and Percentages

Responses	Municipal social worker (N=19)		Municipal doctor (N=19)		Municipal nurse (N=20)		Total
	Freq	%	Freq	%	Freq	%	
Never	7	36.8	2	10.5	3	15.0	12
Sometimes	9	47.4	3	15.8	7	35.0	19
Always	3	15.8	14	73.7	10	50.0	27
Total	19	100.0	19	100.0	20	100.0	58
Pearson Chi-Square=13.51 p<.01							

Table 23-3

The social worker should organize ex-patient groups to improve hospital resources.
Frequencies and Percentages

Responses	Municipal social worker (N=19)		Municipal doctor (N=19)		Municipal nurse (N=20)		Total
	Freq	%	Freq	%	Freq	%	
Never	9	47.4	3	15.0	1	5.0	13
Sometimes	10	52.6	7	35.0	11	55.0	28
Always			10	50.0	8	40.0	18
Total	19	100.0	20	100.0	20	100.0	59
Pearson Chi-Square=18.9 p<.01							

24. The twenty-fourth item in the survey analyzed was the degree to which social workers, doctors, and nurses from both settings agreed that the social worker should give consultation to other professionals on social problems. Table 24-1 shows this analysis.

Table 24-1

The social worker should give consultation to other professionals on social problems of patients.

Responses	Municipal social worker (N=19)		Municipal doctor (N=19)		Municipal nurse (N=20)		Total
	Freq	%	Freq	%	Freq	%	
Never			2	5.1	2	5.0	4
Sometimes	6	15.8	6	15.4	5	12.5	17
Always	32	84.2	31	79.5	33	82.5	96
Total	38	100.0	39	100.0	40	100.0	117
Pearson Chi-Square=2.15 p<.70							

All social workers (N=38), nearly all doctors (N=37), and nearly all nurses (N=38) agreed that the social worker should give consultation to other professionals on social problems of patients.

The difference in the perception of the role of the social worker in giving consultation to other professionals on social problems of patients among social workers, doctors, and nurses was not statistically significant and the Null hypothesis was accepted. Therefore, the hypothesis that doctors and nurses are more likely to perceive the role of the social worker in the emergency room as providing concrete rather than clinical services was not supported.

When the data was divided into two categories, municipal and voluntary, the result shows that all social workers from municipal hospitals (N=19) and social workers from voluntary hospitals (N=19) agreed that the social worker should give consultation to other professionals on social problems of patients. Nearly all doctors from municipal hospitals (N=18) and doctors from voluntary hospitals (N=19) agreed that the social worker should give consultation to other professionals on social problems of patients.

Nearly all nurses from municipal hospitals (N=19) and nurses from voluntary hospitals (N=19) agreed that the social worker should give consultation to other professionals on social problems of patients. A small proportion of doctors from municipal hospitals (N=1) and doctors from voluntary hospitals (N=1) disagreed. An equal number of nurses from municipal hospitals (N=1) and nurses from voluntary hospitals (N=1) disagreed.

The difference in opinions about giving consultation to other professionals on social problems of patients among social workers, doctors, and nurses was not statistically significant and the Null hypothesis was accepted. Therefore, the hypothesis that there will be no significant differences between doctors and nurses in their perception of the role of the social worker in the emergency room in both types of hospitals (municipal and voluntary) was not supported. See tables 24-2, 24-3.

Table 24-2

The social worker should give consultation to other professionals on social problems of patients.

Responses	Municipal social worker (N=19)		Municipal doctor (N=19)		Municipal nurse (N=20)		Total
	Freq	%	Freq	%	Freq	%	
Never			1	5.2	1	5.0	2
Sometimes	2	10.5	1	5.3	3	15.0	6
Always	17	89.5	17	89.5	16	80.0	50
Total	19	100.0	19	100.0	20	100.0	58
Pearson Chi-Square=2.0 p<.73							

Table 24-3

The social worker should give consultation to other professionals on social problems of patients.
Frequencies and Percentages

Responses	Municipal social worker (N=19)		Municipal doctor (N=19)		Municipal nurse (N=20)		Total
	Freq	%	Freq	%	Freq	%	
Never			1	5.0	1	5.0	2
Sometimes	4	21.1	5	25.0	2	10.0	11
Always	15	78.9	14	70.0	17	85.0	46
Total	19	100.0	20	100.0	20	100.0	59
Pearson Chi-Square=2.53 p<.63							

25. The twenty-fifth item in the survey analyzed was the degree to which social workers, doctors, and nurses from both hospitals agreed that the social worker should orient allied health professionals about social work services. Table 25-1 shows this analysis.

Table 25-1

The social worker should orient allied health professionals about social work services,
Frequencies and Percentages

Responses	Municipal social worker (N=19)		Municipal doctor (N=19)		Municipal nurse (N=20)		Total
	Freq	%	Freq	%	Freq	%	
Never	2	5.3			2	5.0	4
Sometimes	8	21.1	8	20.5	7	17.5	23
Always	28	73.7	31	79.5	31	79.5	90
Total	38	100.0	39	100.0	40	100.0	117
Pearson Chi-Square=2.23 p<.69							

Nearly all social workers (N=36), all doctors (N=39), and nearly all nurses (N=38) agreed that the social worker should orient allied health professionals about social work services among social workers, doctors, and nurses was not statistically significant and the Null hypothesis was rejected. Therefore, the hypothesis that doctors and nurses are more likely to perceive the role of the social **worker** in the emergency room as providing concrete rather than clinical services was not supported.

When the data was divided into two categories, municipal and voluntary, the result shows that nearly all social workers from municipal hospitals (N=18) and nearly all social workers from voluntary hospitals (N=18) agreed that the social worker should orient allied health professionals about social work services. All doctors from municipal hospitals (N=19) and all doctors from voluntary hospitals (N=19) agreed that the social worker should orient allied health professionals about social work services. Nearly all nurses from municipal hospitals (N=19) and nearly all nurses from voluntary hospitals (N=19) agreed that the social worker should orient allied health professionals about social work services.

The difference in opinions about orienting allied health professionals about social work services among social workers, doctors, and nurses was not statistically significant in both settings and the Null hypothesis was accepted. Therefore, the hypothesis that there will be no significant differences between doctors and nurses in their perception of the role of the social worker in the emergency room in both types of hospitals (municipal and voluntary) was not supported. See tables 25-2, 25-3.

Table 25-2

The social worker should orient allied health professionals about social work services.
Frequencies and Percentages

Responses	Municipal social worker (N=19)		Municipal doctor (N=19)		Municipal nurse (N=20)		Total
	Freq	%	Freq	%	Freq	%	
Never	1	5.3			1	5.0	2
Sometimes	5	26.3	2	10.5	5	25.0	12
Always	13	68.4	17	89.5	14	70.0	44
Total	19	100.0	19	100.0	20	100.0	58
Pearson Chi-Square=3.08 p<.54							

Table 25-3

The social worker should orient allied health professionals about social work services.
Frequencies and Percentages

Responses	Municipal social worker (N=19)		Municipal doctor (N=19)		Municipal nurse (N=20)		Total
	Freq	%	Freq	%	Freq	%	
Never	1	5.3			1	5.0	2
Sometimes	3	15.8	6	30.0	2	10.0	11
Always	15	78.9	14	70.0	17	85.0	46
Total	19	100.0	20	100.0	20	100.0	59
Pearson Chi-Square=3.58 p<.46							

26. The twenty-sixth item analyzed in the survey was the degree to which social workers, doctors, and nurses from both settings agreed that the social worker should orient residents about social services. Table 26-1 shows this analysis.

Table 26-1

The social worker should orient residents about social services. Frequencies and Percentages

Responses	Municipal social worker (N=19)		Municipal doctor (N=19)		Municipal nurse (N=20)		Total
	Freq	%	Freq	%	Freq	%	
Never			1	2.6	2	5.0	3
Sometimes	9	23.7	6	15.4	6	15.0	21
Always	29	76.3	32	82.1	32	80.0	93
Total	38	100.0	39	100.0	40	100.0	117
Pearson Chi-Square=3.01 p<.55							

All social workers (N=38), nearly all doctors (N=38), and nurses (N=38) agreed that the social worker should orient residents about social services. A small proportion of doctors (N=1) and nurses (N=2) disagreed.

The difference in the perception of the role of the social worker in orienting residents about social services among social workers, doctors, and nurses was not statistically significant and the Null hypothesis was accepted. Therefore, the hypothesis that doctors and nurses are more likely to perceive the role of the social worker in the emergency room as providing concrete rather than clinical services was not supported.

When the data was divided into two categories, municipal and voluntary, the result shows that all social workers from municipal hospitals (N=19), and social workers from voluntary hospitals (N=19) agreed that the social worker should orient residents about social services. All doctors from municipal hospitals (N=19) and nearly all doctors from voluntary hospitals (N=19) agreed that the social worker should orient residents about social services. Nearly all nurses from municipal hospitals (N=19) and nurses from voluntary hospitals (N=19) agreed that the social worker should orient residents about social services.

The difference in opinions about orienting residents about social services among social workers, doctors, and nurses was not statistically significant in both settings and the Null hypothesis was accepted. Therefore, the hypothesis that there will be no significant differences between doctors and nurses in their perception of the role of the social worker in the emergency room in both types of hospitals (municipal and voluntary) was not supported. See tables 26-2, 26-3.

Table 26-2

The social worker should orient residents about social services. Frequencies and Percentages

Responses	Municipal social worker (N=19)		Municipal doctor (N=19)		Municipal nurse (N=20)		Total
	Freq	%	Freq	%	Freq	%	
Never					1	5.0	1
Sometimes	4	21.1	5	26.3	3	15.0	12
Always	15	78.9	14	73.7	16	80.0	45
Total	19	100.0	19	100.0	20	100.0	58
Pearson Chi-Square=2.56 p<.63							

Table 26-3

The social worker should orient residents about social services. Frequencies and Percentages

Responses	Municipal social worker (N=19)		Municipal doctor (N=19)		Municipal nurse (N=20)		Total
	Freq	%	Freq	%	Freq	%	
Never			1	5.0	1	5.0	2
Sometimes	5	26.3	1	5.0	3	15.0	9
Always	14	73.7	18	90.0	16	80.0	48
Total	19	100.0	20	100.0	20	100.0	29
Pearson Chi-Square=4.17 p<.38							

CHAPTER SEVEN

Discussion Of The Findings

This study examines the perceptions that doctors and nurses hold of the role of the social worker in the emergency room and compares them with social workers' self perceptions of what they do. In addition, it examines the relationships between the perceptions of the role of social worker and the type of hospital, municipal or voluntary, where those surveyed work.

The study examined the following hypotheses:

I.   Perceptions of social workers' roles in the medical emergency room will vary significantly by profession: medicine, nursing, and social work.

   a)   Physicians and nurses are more likely to perceive social workers' roles as providing concrete rather than clinical services.
   b)   Social workers perceive their roles as providing both concrete and clinical services.

II.   There will be no significant differences among doctors and nurses in their perceptions of social workers' roles in the emergency room in both types of hospital (municipal or voluntary).

Interpretations, Implications and Future Research Applications

The questionnaire (see appendix A) includes a section on background information or demographics to highlight the characteristics of the respondents. The variables included age, sex, ethnic background, years of emergency room experience, and type of hospital.

Looking at the years of experience, the data show that there were an equal number of social workers, doctors, and nurses with 3 to 10 years of experience in their respective fields. More doctors and nurses were in the over 40 age groups compared to social workers. This could be because social workers started working in the emergency rooms at an early age or due to the of larger number of doctors participating. Regarding the gender of respondents, the result shows that there were more male social worker5 in voluntary hospitals than municipal, more female doctors in voluntary hospitals than municipal, and the same number of female nurses in both settings. The data show that there were more White social workers, doctors, and nurses in municipal hospitals than in voluntary hospitals.

The survey items included in chapter six provided *leading insights* into the *theory of perception* of the social worker's role in the emergency room setting. Perception has been defined by Allport (1955) as the act of understanding events or situations presented. Allport (1955) theorized that bodily needs, rewards, values, personality features and stimuli with emotional content influence what people perceive. It appears that some of the analytical tools used in the survey lead to specific implications and inferences that should be used in future determination of the social worker's role in the emergency room setting. In this section each of the clinical and concrete survey questions are analyzed using current theories of social work. Crisis intervention theory is important because patients enter the emergency room in crisis. Role theory provides a method of description and analysis of the behavior of people in organizations. Each question has been presented in chapter six using statistical tables 1-1 through 26-3.

Tables 1-1 through tables 1-3 refer to the concrete services of the social worker's role in determining eligibility of patients for social services in the emergency room setting. The data show that doctors and nurses in municipal and voluntary hospitals are unanimously against social worker in the emergency room determining eligibility of patients for social services. The doctors and nurses surveyed believe that medical care is the only long-term or short-term need of the emergency room patient. But medical treatment may not be the only need a patient has. After emergency care, the patient may need to be offered assistance with concrete tasks, such as facilitating a return home in a domestic violence situation. Doctors and nurses who provide emergency medical care need to refer patients to a social worker for post-trauma social services.

Although the role of the social worker is unclear in post-trauma situations, more education and reinforcement about the social worker's role in emergency room is a critical factor in enabling doctors and nurses to become advocates for patients who need social services. The social worker's role in providing concrete services is unclear even to social workers in both municipal and voluntary hospital. This leads to the finding that continuing education for social workers in emergency settings is needed. Education could emphasize not only the functions of social work in emergency room settings but also teach the skills needed to demonstrate and communicate those functions to others.

Tables 2-1 through 2-3 refers to the concrete services of the social worker's role in helping patients obtain medical appliances. Doctors, nurses, and social workers in both hospital settings agree that the social worker should help patients obtain medical appliances.

Tables 3-1 through 3-3 refer to the concrete service of the social worker's role in interpreting feelings of patients to physicians. Although there is no statistical significance, a slight majority of doctors and nurses agreed that the social worker should always interpret feelings of patients to physicians. Social workers are better qualified and more apt to identify and assess social issues and social problems of patients than doctors and nurses are. When the patient arrives in the emergency room he/she made bring a number of social or psychological problems that should be part of an overall assessment of medical needs.

Tables 4-1 through 4-3, and tables 5-1 through 5-3, refer to the concrete services reporting patients' medical problems to physicians, and symptoms to physicians. The data show that social workers, doctors, and nurses in voluntary hospitals agree that the social worker should report patient's medical problems and symptoms to physicians. One role of the social worker in the emergency room is to facilitate the transmission of patients' complaints to emergency room medical personnel. The social worker is trained to observe and assess the patients' demeanor on arrival at the emergency room and present this assessment to the doctor or nurse. The social worker may not ask specific clinical questions but can focus on primary intervention.

Tables 6-1 through 6-3, refer to the concrete services of the social worker's role in explaining physicians' orders to patients. The data show that social workers, doctors, and nurses were in statistical agreement that the social worker should explain physicians' orders. The social worker can assist patients in understanding treatment plans and making follow-up appointments as well as making resources in the social work department available to them

Tables 7-1 through 7-3 refer to the concrete services of the social worker's role in acting as liaison between doctor and patients. The data show that nearly all social workers, doctors, and nurses in both hospital settings agree that the social worker should function as liaison between doctors and patients.

Tables 8-1 through 8-3 refer to the clinical services of the social worker in collaborating with other professionals on plan for patients' care. The data show that social workers, doctors, and nurses from both hospital settings agree that the social worker should collaborate with other professionals on plans for patients' care. The rationale for social work participation in collaborative activities is based on the recognition of the complexity of human problems and the high degree of knowledge, technology, and skills needed to meet them. The natures of crisis that lead patients to emergency rooms present many opportunities for collaboration between social workers and physicians. This can lead to increased efficiency in the emergency room and keep patients from slipping through the cracks of the health care system. The concept of social workers as having many important roles in the emergency room is not new. *Abramson & Mizrah, (1987) noted that there are many ways in which social workers provide assistance to physicians in relation to patient care by providing clinical and concrete services, in assisting patients coping with crisis, such as sudden death, domestic violence, child abuse, elderly abuse, homelessness, substance abuse, and issues of discharge planning.*

Tables 9-1 through 9-3 and tables 10-1 through 10-3 refer to the clinical services of the social worker's role in diagnosing social problems of patients and determining patients' need for social services. The data show that social workers, doctors, and nurses in both municipal and voluntary hospitals were in statistical agreement that the social worker should diagnose the social problems of patients. Social workers can assist in identification and reduction of health risks with individuals and more generally in a community. Social work in health care is multidimensional-not only is it bio psychosocial but it is fully social-environmental as well. *These dimensions are critical in shaping the future development of social work practice and they will affect the roles of research and education as the practice evolves (Epstein, 1995). This study provides strong support for the active role of the social worker in the emergency room in acting as liaison between doctors and patients in the emergency room.*

Tables 11-1 through 11-3 refer to the clinical services of the social worker's role in recommending treatment for mentally ill patients. The data show that social workers, doctors, and nurses in municipal and voluntary hospitals were in statistical agreement that the social worker should recommend treatment for mentally ill patients. Social workers provide psychosocial intervention for psychologically vulnerable populations. It is essential for social workers to intervene directly in the family system, not only with a family group, not only with the patient but also with caregivers. The objective of interventions are always to reduce the years of mentally unhealthy life and enhance the years of mental healthy life. This goes beyond medical notions of mental health as simply the lack of mental illness (Rehr, Rosemberg, & Blumenfields, 1998). Further research is needed to find out why more social workers, doctors, and nurses in voluntary hospitals responded that the social worker should never recommend treatment for mentally ill patients.

Tables 12-1 through 12-3, refer to the concrete services of the social worker's role in strengthening patients' participation in their own care. The data show that social workers, doctors, and nurses from both hospital settings agree that the social worker should provide this service. Patients who participate in their medical treatment develop healthier with regard to the role of the social worker in strengthening patients' participation in their own care. Client empowerment is key to health promotion and prevention, both, to engage individuals in developing healthier lifestyles and are more apt to become active members of the "body politic," confident and capable of impacting the development of policies and progress of the society to ensure that all citizens enjoy the social supports they require to realize their potential (Cowless, 2000).

Tables 13-1 through 13-3 refers to the clinical services of the social worker's role in helping patients overcome personal crisis. The data show that social workers, doctors, and nurses in both settings agree that the social worker should provide this service. Some common bio-psychosocial problems that social workers can help to address in the emergency room include drug and alcohol abuse, child abuse and neglect, domestic violence, elder abuse, teenage pregnancy, sexually transmitted diseases, suicide, depression, homicide, obsessive- compulsive behaviors, panic disorders, agoraphobia, social isolation, emotional withdrawal, and self-mutilation behavior (Cowles, 2000). Tables 14-1 through 14-3, refer to the concrete services of the social worker's role in encouraging patients to follow medical recommendations. The data show that social workers, doctors, and nurses in both hospital settings agree that the social worker should encourage patients to follow medical recommendations. This type of concrete social work service can be cost-effective for the hospital (Ponto and Berg, 1992) and more effective for the patients, who otherwise tend to keep coming back to the emergency room for treatment.

Tables 15-1 through 15-3 refer to the clinical services of the social worker's role in providing emotional support to patients. The data show that all social workers, and nearly all doctors, and nurses were in both hospital settings agree that the social worker should provide this service. *Clinical social work interventions may be directed to either physical, psychological, or social comfort and function aspects by addressing (1) barriers to admission to the hospital; (2) problems of adjustment lo the hospital; (3) problems of adjusting to the diagnosis, prognosis, or treatment plan; (4) lack of information to make informed decisions and to feel in control; (5) lack of resources to meet needs; and (6) barriers to discharge (Cowles, 2000).*

Tables 16-1 through 16-3 refers to the clinical services of the social worker's role in helping patients adjust to illness. The data show that social workers, doctors, and nurses in both hospital settings agree that the social worker should provide this service. Often times, the diagnosis, prognosis, or treatment plan requires major changes in the lives of patients and their family members. The effects usually are both emotional and socio- environmental. For example, patients who learn they have a health problem that will require them to quit working or change the nature of their work may face both economic problems and emotional reactions. This is an example of a "psycho-social" problem because it has both emotional and social environmental components. Professional social workers are well suited to the provision of this clinical service (Cowless, 2000), (Cowles, 2000). This is a clinical service.

Tables 17-1 through 17-3 and tables 18-1 through 18-3 refer to the clinical services of the social worker's role in providing psychotherapy to emotionally disturbed patients, and using psychotherapeutic techniques with patients. The data show that more social workers than doctors and nurses agree that this is a service that should be provided by the social worker. This study indicates that doctors and nurses do not view social workers as competent to provide clinical services to emotionally disturbed patients. Education would emphasized not only the content of social work functions in hospital settings but also provide the skills to demonstrate and communicate those functions to others.

Tables 19-1 through 19-3 refer to the concrete service of the social worker's role in providing post-hospital employment counseling to patients. The data show that more doctors and nurses than social workers were in statistical agreement in voluntary hospitals only. The data show that more doctors and nurses than social workers agree that the social worker should provide employment counseling. This author believes that more continuing education for social workers would emphasize not only the content of social work functions in the emergency room but also it would demonstrate and communicate those functions to others.

Tables 20-1 through 20-3 refer to the concrete service of the social worker's role in conducting pre-discharge study of homes. The data show that more doctors and nurses than social workers agree that the social worker should provide this service. More social workers from municipal hospitals than from voluntary hospitals think that the social worker should conduct pre-discharge studies of homes. This study indicates that the social worker's role is unclear to social workers in both hospital settings. The author believes that more education for social workers in emergency room settings should be provided. Education would emphasize not only the content of social work functions in hospital settings, but also the skills to demonstrate and communicate those functions to others.

Tables 21-1 through 21-3 refer to the concrete service of the social worker's role in referring families to community agencies. The data show that there were no significant differences among social workers, doctors, and nurses in both hospital settings. All agree that the social worker should provide this service. Common social work services in hospital emergency rooms include brief counseling and referral and resource finding for patients and families with such presenting problems as victims of disasters, evictions from their homes. Such social work services can be cost-effective for the hospital (Ponto & Berg, 1992).

Tables 22-1 through 22-3 and tables 23-1 through 23-3 refer to the concrete services of the social worker's role in interpreting hospital services to community agencies and organizing ex-patient groups to improve hospital resources. The data show that nearly all social workers, doctors, and nurses in both hospital settings agree that the social worker should interpret hospital services to community agencies. Many people, especially elderly people with functional impairments do not know what hospital services are available to them, or are reluctant to ask for help (Blazer, 1988). The, the emergency room social worker can help ensure that the community has information of hospital's services through, for example, the mass media, physicians, hospital emergency rooms and direct patient education.

More nurses and social workers than doctors agree that the social worker should organize ex-patient groups to improve hospital resources. The survey shows that the social worker's role is unclear in this regard to social workers in both hospital settings. The author believes that more continuing education for social workers in emergency room settings should be provided.

Tables 24-1 through 24-3 refer to the concrete services of the social worker's role in giving consultation to other professionals on social problems of patients. The data show that nearly all social workers, doctors, and nurses in both hospital settings agree that this service should be provided by the social worker. Social workers enhance physicians' effectiveness with patients by sharing knowledge about the cultural and environmental backgrounds of patients. In doing so, a larger number of patients may be treated within the limited time available; thus maximizing the income derived from treatment.

Tables 25-1 through 25-3 refer to the clinical services of the social worker's role in orienting allied health professionals about social work services. The data show that nearly all social workers, doctors, and nurses in both hospital settings agree that the social worker should orient allied health professionals abut social work services. Lack of understanding of social workers' roles may prevent doctors and nurses from referring patients experiencing medical emergencies for social work intervention. Social workers must be capable of explaining with clarity the importance of their clinical services to medical staff and hospital administrators (Cheethan, Fuller, McVor, 1992.)

Tables 26-1 through 26-3 refer the clinical services of the social worker's role in orienting residents about social services. The data show that nearly all social workers, doctors, and nurses in both hospital settings agree that the social worker should orient residents about social work services. Persons outside the profession may not be familiar with the range of services and skills offered by social workers. Lack of knowledge of what social workers do creates a conflict in collaborating with other professionals in the provision of services.

Theoretical Interpretation of Findings

The major findings of this study, in terms of hypotheses tested is that there are differences among social workers, doctors, and nurses in their perceptions of the role of the social worker in the emergency room. This study also confirms the hypothesis that social workers perceive their roles as providing both concrete and clinical services. The findings are consistent with Carrigan's (1974) survey of hospital workers' perception of social work practice in health care settings.

The results of this study illustrated here reiterate those described in the literature reviewed from 1967 through 2000. This could be due to organizational factors affecting the delivery of social work services in the emergency room setting. However, the findings also seem to reflect a degree of role ambiguity vis-a-vis the social worker in the emergency room. The findings in this study indicate that this is still a critical issue, as doctors and nurses generally do not view social workers as competent to diagnose emotional problems, use psychotherapeutic techniques, or provide psychotherapy to emotionally disturbed patients.

The seeds for a disagreement that linger today between physicians and social workers concerning the social worker's role in the emergency room are evident when other expectations are compared even in very early studies. Cabot (1928) expected the role of the social worker to resolve around "bridging the gap" between the hospital environment and the usual social environment of the patients in order to remove barriers to effective medical treatment, while Cannon (1923) additionally expected the hospital social worker role to include efforts to modify any social environmental or emotional causes or effects of the patients' health condition.

Interdisciplinary experiences will not bear positive results if other professionals do not recognize social workers' unique authority or expertise and do not share the social work profession's perceptions of its domain. Medicine, as an autonomous profession, within the constraints imposed by bureaucracy, heads a hierarchy of disciplines of lower status. The unequal power bases of the health care profession lead to the designation of handmaiden roles and precludes participation in a truly collaborative process (Cowles, 2000).

The emergency room social worker is a specialist that is fully trained and qualified to provide emergency care at several levels to the patient using the "here and now" approach. In the emergency room, the primary role of the social worker involves crisis intervention. The social worker looks for the underlying causes of the presenting problem, meaning what happened in the patient's life that has caused a crisis. Whatever the nature of the crisis that speeds an emergency room visit- whether it's a sudden illness, exacerbation of chronic illness, failure of psychological defenses, collapse of social supports, or abuse- the patient has come to the emergency room for immediate relief.

This type of social worker is so specialized in a very small part of the hospital that doctors and nurses have unclear perceptions of his/her role. The emergency room social worker strikes a very fine balance between the clinical and the social aspects of patient care. This social worker is unique in providing care at the most difficult and sophisticated level, and is far more trained in crisis intervention. This study is limited to perceptions of social workers, doctors, and nurses about the role of the social worker in the emergency room. Another limitation is that this was a study of perceptions rather than observed behavior. The sample was self-selected and the study sites were chosen on the basis of convenience. Additional limitations include that it was a one-time basis survey, a one-group study design. and these factors decrease the ability to generalize from this data to the larger population.

Implications for further Research

This study supports the concern reflected in the descriptive literature regarding the role of the social worker in the hospital emergency room, and thereby raises a number of empirical questions to be addressed. Are the findings of this study peculiar to place? All of the social workers, doctors, and nurses who participated in this study were from medical emergency rooms. It would therefore be interesting to replicate this study or design similar studies for social workers, doctors, and nurses practicing in psychiatric emergency rooms in order to test the generalizability of the findings.

Implications for Social Work Education

Social work students need to acquire both knowledge and skills that will make it possible for them to carry out their role, as well as a sense of identification with and commitment to the profession. This study suggests that social **work** interventions are needed to address patients' health behavior and to promote the creation and maintenance of social support. This study also provides a better understanding of the need for stronger support for social workers in the emergency room so they may help other emergency room staff more fully serve the needs of the community.

The need is growing for all hospital staff, including social workers to demonstrate "their effectiveness" if they hope to retain their positions in the field. Social work educators recognize this need and can help students demonstrate and communicate their skills levels to medical and nursing staff.

Implications for Social Policy

This study will contribute to social policy in its recognition of the need to inform and educate health care professionals and administrators about the range of skills and roles that should be performed by social workers in the emergency room. In addition, this research can be used to indicate the extent to which social workers are being fully utilized in hospital emergency rooms. The data from this study can be used to better advocate for social workers in emergency room settings and to help those in these settings understand the obstacles they face in working with their colleagues.

This study contributes to an understanding of the roles and the range of skills of social work in hospital medical emergency rooms. As managed care becomes a dominant mode of health care delivery, it will be increasingly important for health care administrators to fully utilize the skills of professional staff (Cowless, 2000). The funding of social workers in the emergency room setting is often at risk. It is very rare indeed for a patient to come to the emergency room for care only because he/she needs the assistance of a social worker. But it is quite possible that the medical problems which brought that person to the emergency room may cause psychosocial problems as well; and the care provided for that medical problem may actually lead to problems in other areas-psychosocial problems (Auslander, 2000). Like any other members of the staff, the social worker is expected to cooperate in the emergency room's efforts to advance and maintain its own well-being.

Skilled social workers are cost-effective, physician-extenders in the emergency room where to the hospital's benefit, they provide enhanced services and ensure access to care for community residents (Harrington, 1991). It is well known that noninsured patients, or social admissions ties up beds and are expensive for hospitals. Social admissions are patients who do not need hospital-level care, but cannot easily be sent home or to alternate care providers. When social workers reduce social admissions, they are helping reduce the cost of emergency medical care for everyone.

The emergency room social worker exemplifies, in a crisis- oriented context, the ability of social workers to make a difference. This includes situations where patients and families have physical, environmental, and emotional needs.

In summation, social work services in the hospital medical emergency rooms are beneficial for the following reasons:

a) Reduction in social admissions.
b) Increased community access to services.
c) Increased community confidence.
d) Continue low lengths-of-stay.
e) Quicker identification and amelioration of problem situations.
f) Maximization of physician and nurse time in the emergency room.

All of these advantages gained from social work services in the emergency room are likely to be cost-effective for the hospitals in the short term, and have the potential for providing hospitals enormous cost-benefits for clients and communities. The challenge for social workers is to demonstrate the relevance of their expertise to the enhancement of patient care in complex hospital systems.

Social workers will need to educate physicians and other health care professionals about their contributions to patient care and to system efficiency to achieve this objective. Education would emphasized not only the content of social work roles in emergency room settings, but also the skills to demonstrate and communicate those roles to physicians and other health care professionals.

Social workers must use hindsight to reflect on the evolution of roles and functions and insight to develop a new understanding of relationships with other health care professionals. They may with foresight and careful analysis and planning, establish a clearer domain for social work in health care (Davison, 1990).

REFERENCES

Arndt, E., & Duchemin, K. (1995). More than bandaids: Emotional support and education during the downsizing process. Paper presented at the International Conference on Social Work in Health and Mental Health. Jerusalem, Israel. January, 1995.

Abramson, J.S., & Mizrahi, T. (1987). Strategies for enhancing collaboration between social workers and physicians. *Social Work in Health Care*, 12, 1-21.

Abramson, J., & Mizrahi, T. (] 996). When social workers and physicians collaborate: Positive and negative interdisciplinary experiences. *Journal of the National Association of Social Workers*, 4, 24-28.

Abramson, J. S.,& Rosenthal, B.(1995). Collaboration: Interdisciplinary and interorganizational application. *Encyclopedia of social work.* Washington, DC: NASW Press.

Aghababian, R., & McQuaide, D.S. (1992). *Emergency medicine.* Boston: Little, Brown.

Allport, F. H. (1955). *Theories of perception and the concept of structure.* New York: John Wiley & Sons.

American Hospitals Association (1961). *Essentials of a service department and related institutions.* Chicago: Author.

Aradine, C., & Pridrnan, K. F. (1973). Model collaboration. *Nursing Outlook*, 21, 10.

Atkatz, J. (1994). *Discharge planning for homeless patients: A social work practice dilemma.* Unpublished doctoral dissertation, Yeshiva University, New York.

Auslander, G., Auslander, G. K., & Schneiman, G. (1996). Clients' views of social work services in the hospital setting in Israel. *Social Work in Health Care, 22,* 57-68.

Auslander, G. K. (2000). Outcomes of social **work** intervention in health care settings. *Social Work in Health Care,* 31 (2), 31-46.

Austin, D. M. (1995). Management overview: Characteristics of human services organizations. *Encyclopedia of social work, 19th ed.,* (pp. 1642-1656). Washington, DC: NASW Press.

Barker, R.L. (1995). *The social work dictionary, 4th ed.* Washington DC: NASW Press. Baxt, W. G. (2000). Crisis at America's teaching hospitals. *Annals of Emergency Medicine, 36,* 145-148. Benett, M. J. (1973). The social worker's role: Emergency medical services. *Hospitals, Journal of the American Hospital Association, 41,* 11-19.

Berger, C., Cayner, J., Jensen, G.• Mizrahi, T., Sceny, A., & Trachtenberg, J. (1996). The changing scene of social work in hospitals: A report of a national study by the Society for Social Work Administrators in Health Care and NASW. *Health and Social Work, 21,* 167-176.

Bergman, A. (1976). Emergency room: A role for social workers. *Health and Social Work, 1,* 33-44.

Blazer, D. (1988). Home health care: House calls revisited. *American Journal of Public Health, 78,* (30), 238-239.

Borzo, G. (1993). More patients using emergency rooms for non-emergency problems. American Medical News, 31, 459-465.

Cummings, K. C., & Abell, **R. M.** (1993). Losing sight of the shore: How a future integrated American health care organization might look. *Health Care Management Review,* **18,** 39-50.

Campton, B. R., & Galaway, 8. (1989). Theoretical perspectives for social work practice. *Social work process,* (pp. 123-141). Belmont, CA: Wadsworth

Carrasquillo, O., Himmelstein, D. U., Woolhandler, S., & Bor, D. H. (1999). A reappraisal of private employers' role in providing health insurance. *New England Journal of Medicine,* 340, 109-114.

Caplan, G. (1964). *Principles of preventive psychiatry.* New York: Basic Books. Caplan, G. (1974). Support systems and community mental health. New York: Basic Books.

Carrigan, Z. H. (1974). *The effect of professional role position on the perception of interdisciplinary social work practice in health care settings.* Unpublished doctoral dissertation. The Catholic University of America, Washington, DC.

Cheetham, J., Fuller, R., McVor, G., & McVor, J. () 992). *Evaluating social work effectiveness.* Bristol, PA: Aspen University Press.

Cowles, L. A., & Lefcowitz, M. (1992). Interdisciplinary expectations of the medical social worker in the hospital setting. *Health and Social Work,* 17 (1), 57-65.

Cowles, L.A. (2000). *Social work in the healthfield: A care perspective.* New York: The Haworth Press.

Clement, J., & Klinbeil, K. S. (1981). The emergency room. *Health and Social Work,* 3, **83-88.**

Dalen, E. J. (2000). Health care in America: The good, the bad, and the ugly. *Archives of Internal Medicine,* 160, 2573-2576.

Davidson, K. (1998). Educating students for social work in health care today. In Scharness, Gerald and Lightbum, Anita (Eds.), Humane managed care. Washington, DC: NASW Press, 425-429.

Davidson, K. (1990). Role blurring and the hospital social worker's search for a clear domain. *Health and Social Work,* 15, 228-234. Douglas, R. L., & Torres, R. E. (1994). Evaluation of a managed care program for the non-Medicaid urban poor. *Journal of Health Care for the Poor and Underserved,* 5, 83-96.

Duncan, W. C., & Machanon, B. (1981). *Preventive and community medicine.* Chicago: University of Chicago Press.

Dziegielewski, S. F. (1998). The changing face of health care social work: Professional practice in the era of managed care. *Springer series on social work.* 3, 3-16.

Egan, M., & Kadushin, G. (1995). Competitive allies: Rural nurses' and social workers' perceptions of the role of the social worker in the hospital setting. *Social Work in Health Care,* 20, 1-20.

Ell, K. (1995). Crisis intervention: Research needs. *Encyclopedia of social work, 18th ed.,* (pp. 660-665). Washington, DC: **NASW** Press. Elliot, M. (1987). Roles and functions of social work. *Encyclopedia of social work, 18th ed,* (pp. 500-502). Washington, DC: NASW Press.

Epstein, I. (1995). Promoting reflective social work education. In P. Hess & E. Mullen (Eds.). *Practice research partnership*. Washington, DC: NASW Press.

Gibelman, M. (1995). *What social workers do*. Washington, DC: NASW Press. Golan, N. (1978). *Crisis intervention*. New York: Free Press.

Grumbach, K. (2000). Insuring the uninsured: Time to end the aura of invisibility. *Journal of the American Medical Association*, 284, No. 16, 2114-2116.

Harrington, D.V. (1991). The ER social worker: Cost effective, crisis oriented discharge planning-and more *Social Work and Discharge Planning*. Cape Cod Hospital 8-10. Hyannis, MA.

Hendricks, J. B. (1991). *Crisis intervention in criminal justice*. Springfield, IL: Sage Publications.

Hepworth, D. H., & Larsen, J. (1993). Direct social work practice. *Theory and skills, 4th ed.*. Pacific Grove, CA: Brooks/Cole.

Joint Commission on Accreditation of Health Care Organizations (1998). *Accreditation manual for hospitals*. Chicago: Author.

Kadushin, G. (1996). Elderly hospitalized patients' perception of the interaction with the social worker during discharge planning. *Social Work in Health Care*, 23, 1-19.

Keehn, D. Roglitz, C., & Bowden, L. M. (1994). Impact of social work recidivism and non-medical complaints in the emergency department. *Social Work in Health Care*, 23, 65-74.

Knopp, R. K., Biros, M. H., White, J. D., & Waeckerle, J. F. (2000). The uninsured: Medicine's challenge to our political leaders. *Annals of Emergency Medicine*, 35, 295-297.

Koeske, G. F., Koeske, D., & Mallinger, L. (1993). Perceptions of professional competence: Cross-disciplinary ratings of psychologists, social workers, and psychiatrists. *American Journal of Orthopsychiatry*, 63, 45-52.

Kotellchuck, R. (1994). *The New York City health care system: A paradigm under siege*, (pp.21-33). New York: The Haworth Press, Inc.

Krauss, B., & Zurakowski, D. (1998). Sedation patterns in pediatric and general community hospital emergency departments. *Pediatric Emergency Care*, 14, 99-103.

Kuttner, R. (1999). The American health care system: Health insurance coverage. *New England Journal of Medicine,* 340, 163-168.

Lindemann, E. (1965). Symptomatology and management of acute grief. In H.J. Parad (Ed.), *Crisis intervention: Selected readings,* (pp. 7-21). New York: Family Service Association of America.

MacEachron, A. (1995). Experimental and quasi-experimental research desing. *Encyclopedia of social work, 19th ed.,* (pp. 909-916). Washington, D.C: NASW Press.

McCulloch. J. W., & Brown, J. J. (1970). Social work in general medical practice. *Medical Social Work,* 22, 30.

McNeil, T., Nicholas, D., Szechy, K., & Lac L.(1998). Perceived outcome of social work intervention: Beyond consumer information. *Social Work in Health Care,* 26, 1-18.

Merton, R. (1957). *Social theory and social structure.* New York: Free Press.

Mizrahi, T. (1995). Health care: Reform initiatives. *Encyclopedia of social work, 19th ed,* (pp. 1185-1196). Washington, DC: NASW Press.

Mizrahi, T., & Abramson. J. (1985). Sources of strain between physicians and social workers: Implications for social workers in health care settings. *Social Work in Health Care,* 10, 33-5 I.

Mizrahi, T. & Abramson, J. (2000). Collaboration - between social workers and physicians: Perspectives on a shared case. *Social Work in Health Care,* 31, 3.

National Allied Health Casemix Committee (1997). *Australian allied health classification system.* Version one. Australia: Author.

National Center for Health Statistics (2000). *Emergency room users.* Washington, DC: Author.

Oberhofer Dane, B., & Simon. B. L. (1990). Resident guests: Social workers in host settings. *Social Work,* 36, 208-211.

O'Boyle, C. M., Davis, K. D., Russo, B. A., & Kraf, T. J. (1985). Emergency care: The first 24 hours. Norwalk, CT: Appleton Century Crofts.

Olsen. R., & Olsen, M. (1967). Role expectations and perceptions of social workers in medical settings. *Social Work,* 12, 70-78.

Parad, H.J. (1965). A framework for studying families in crisis. *Social Work,* 5, 18-21.

Parad, H. J., & Parad, L. G. (1990). *Crisis intervention.* Milwaukee: Families International Service Association of America.

Phillips, B., McCulloch, J. W., Brown, M. J., & Hambro, N. (1971). Social Work and Medical Practice. Studies in the United States and Great Britain indicate physicians' incomplete understanding of the function of social work services. Hospitals, J.A.H. 45, 76-79.

Poindexter, C. C. (1997). In the aftermath: Serial crisis intervention for people with HIV. *Health and Social Work,* 22, 125-131.

Ponto, J.M., & Berg, W. (1992). Social work services in the emergency department: A cost-benefit analysis of an extended coverage program *Health and Social Work,* 17, 66-72.

Rachman, R. (1997). Hospital social work and community care: The practitioners' view. In G.K. Auslander (Ed.), International Perspectives on social work in health care (pp.211-222). New York: The Haworth Press, Inc.

Rapoport, L. (1965). The state of crisis: Some theoretical considerations. In H.J. Parad (Ed.), Crisis intervention: *Selected readings,* (pp. 265-31). New York: Family service Association of America.

Rapoport, L. (1970). Crisis intervention as a mode of brief treatment. In R. Roberts & R. Nee (Eds.), *Theories of social casework,* (pp. 265-312). Chicago: University of Chicago Press.

Rehr, H., Blumenfield, S., & Rosenberg, G. (1998). *Creative social work in health care: Clients, the community, and your organization.* New York: The Mount Sinai Medical Center Press. Rizzo, V., & Abrams, A. (2000). Utilization review: A powerful social work role in health care settings. *Health and Social Work,* 25, 264-269.

Roberts, A. R. (1990). Crisis intervention handbook: Assessment treatment and research. Belmont, CA: Wadsworth.

Rubin, A., & Babbie, E. (1997). *Research methods for social work.* Belmont, CA: Wadsworth.

Rubin Wainrib, B., & Bloch, L. (1999). *Crisis intervention and trauma response: Theory and practice.* New York: Springer Publishing.

Sarbin, T. R. (1954). Role theory. In L. Gardner, (Ed.), *Handbook of social psychology.* Reading, MA: Adisson-Wesley Publishers.

Schamess G., & Lightbum, A. (Eds.), *Humane managed care,* (pp. 425-429). Washington, DC: NASW Press.

Schwarts, G. M., Safar, P., & Wagner, D. K. (1986). *Principles and practice of emergency medicine, 2nd ed.,* (pp. 1-11). W.B. SAunders Co. Philadelphia, PA.

Sherer, R. A. (1999). More managed care means less charity care. *Psychiatric Times Vol. XVI, No. 12.*

Side V. W. (1990). A socialist perspective of the US health care system. New York: Basic Books.

Skidmore, R. A., Thackeray, M. G., & Farley, 0. W. (1997). *Introduction to social work, 1hed.* Boston: Allyn & Bacon.

Soskis, C. (1985). *Social work in the emergency room.* New York: Springer Publishing.

SPSS Base 9.0 (1999). *Applications guide.* Chicago: SPSS, Inc.

Wrenn, K., & Rice, N. (1993). Social work services in an emergency department: An integral part of the health care safety net. *Academy of Emergency Medicine,* 1, 247-253. XVI, 12.

APPENDIX A

Physician and Nurse Questionnaire

Part I: Social Work Activities

Directions: Below is a list of social work activities or functions related to patients care and rehabilitation. You are being asked to indicate how you think those activities should be carried out by social workers. Please circle the appropriate number to the right of the task that best represents how often social workers **should be** responsible for carrying out the task. Use the coding system below:

1. NEVER OR RARELY done by social workers (less than 5% of the time)
2. SELDOM done by social workers (about 25% of the time)
3. SOMETIMES done by social workers (about 50% of the time)
4. OFTEN done by social workers (about 75% of the time)
5. ALWAYS OR NEARLY ALWAYS done by social workers (more than 95% of the time)

THE SOCIAL WORKER SHOULD:

Never or Rarely 1	Seldom 2	Sometimes 3	Often 4	Always or Nearly Always 5

1. Determine eligibility of patients	1 2 3 4 5
2. Educate patients about hospital services	1 2 3 4 5
3. Help patients obtain medical appliances	1 2 3 4 5
4. Interpret feelings of patients to physicians	1 2 3 4 5
5. Report emotional changes to physicians	1 2 3 4 5
6. Report patients' medical problems to physicians	1 2 3 4 5
7. Report patients' medical symptoms to physicians	1 2 3 4 5
8. Explain physicians' orders to patients	1 2 3 4 5
9. Act as liaison between doctor and patients	1 2 3 4 5
10. Collaborate with other professionals on plan for patients care	1 2 3 4 5
11. Screen patients for psychiatric evaluation	1 2 3 4 5
12. Appraise patient's emotional needs	1 2 3 4 5
13. Diagnose social problems of patients	1 2 3 4 5
14. Determine patients' need for social services	1 2 3 4 5
15. Determine type of extended care needed by patients	1 2 3 4 5
16. Recommend treatment for mentally ill patients	1 2 3 4 5
17. Recommend treatment for patients' emotional problems	1 2 3 4 5
18. Strengthen patients' participation in their own care	1 2 3 4 5
19. Help patients Overcome personal crises	1 2 3 4 5

20. Help patients to Overcome negative feelings about treatment	1 2 3 4 5
21. Encourage patients to follow medical recommendations	1 2 3 4 5
22. Help patients to overcome emotional barriers to discharge	1 2 3 4 5
23. Help patients to overcome emotional barriers to treatment	1 2 3 4 5
24. Provide emotional support to patient	1 2 3 4 5
25. Help patients adjust to separation from families	1 2 3 4 5
26. Help patients adjust to chronic conditions	1 2 3 4 5
27. Help patient's Adjust to treatment setting!	1 2 3 4 5
28. Help patient adjust to illness	1 2 3 4 5
29. Provide psychotherapy to emotionally disturbed patients	1 2 3 4 5
30. Use psychotherapeutic techniques with patients	1 2 3 4 5
31. Prepare family for return of patient	1 2 3 4 5
32. Help patients to improve relations with family	1 2 3 4 5
33. Help families with patients' medical problems	1 2 3 4 5
34. Provide post-hospital employment counseling to patients	1 2 3 4 5
35. Conduct pre-discharge study of homes	1 2 3 4 5
36. Make provisions for patient care in community	1 2 3 4 5
37. Make referrals of patients to community agencies	1 2 3 4 5
38. Provide case consultation to other agencies about patients	1 2 3 4 5
39. Refer families to community agencies	1 2 3 4 5
40. Obtain information on community resourcesa	1 2 3 4 5

Never or Rarely 1	Seldom 2	Sometimes 3	Often 4	Always or Nearly Always 5

41. Act as an advocate in securing community resources for patient	1 2 3 4 5
42. Obtain volunteer resources from community	1 2 3 4 5
43. Interpret hospital services to the community	1 2 3 4 5
44. Interpret hospital services to community agencies	1 2 3 4 5
45. Organize ex-patient groups to improve hospital resources	1 2 3 4 5
46. Orient allied health professionals on psychosocial needs of patients	1 2 3 4 5
47. Give consultation to other professionals on social problems of patients	1 2 3 4 5
48. Orient allied health professionals about social work services	1 2 3 4 5
49. Orient residents about social work services	1 2 3 4 5

Part II: Background Information

1. *Your age:*
   1 - Less than 30
   2 - 31-35
   3 - 36-40
   4 - 41-45
   5 - 46-50
   6 - 51-55
   7 - 56-50
   8 - 60 or over

2. *Sex:*
   1 - Male
   2 - Female

3. *Ethnic Background:*
   1 - White non-Hispanic
   2 - Hispanic
   3 - African-American
   4 - Other, please specify:

4. *Highest Degree:*
   1 - Associate
   2 - Bachelors
   3 - Masters
   4 - Doctorate

5. *Years of emergency
   room experience:*
   1 - Less than 3
   2 - 3-5
   3 - 6-10
   4 - 11-15
   5 - 16 or more

6. *Type of control of hospital in which yo u are
   presently employed:*
   1 - Municipal
   2 - Voluntary not-for-profit

Part I: Social Work Activities

Directions: Below is a list of social work activities or functions related to patients care and rehabilitation. You are being asked to indicate how you think those activities should be carried out by social workers. Please circle the appropriate number to the right of the task that best represents how often social workers **should be** responsible for carrying out the task. Use the coding system below:

1. NEVER OR RARELY done by social workers (less than 5% of the time)
2. SELDOM done by social workers (about 25% of the time)
3. SOMETIMES done by social workers (about 50% of the time)
4. OFTEN done by social workers (about 75% of the time)
5. ALWAYS OR NEARLY ALWAYS done by social workers (more than 95% of the time)

THE SOCIAL WORKER SHOULD:

1. Determine eligibility of patients	**1 2 3 4 5**
2. Educate patients about hospital services	**1 2 3 4 5**
3. Help patients obtain medical appliances	**1 2 3 4 5**
4. Interpret feelings of patients to physicians	**1 2 3 4 5**
5. Report emotional changes to physicians	**1 2 3 4 5**
6. Report patients' medical problems to physicians	**1 2 3 4 5**
7. Report patients' medical symptoms to physicians	**1 2 3 4 5**
8. Explain physicians' orders to patients	**1 2 3 4 5**
9. Act as liaison between doctor and patients	**1 2 3 4 5**
10. Collaborate with other professionals on plan for patients care	**1 2 3 4 5**
11. Screen patients for psychiatric evaluation	**1 2 3 4 5**

12. Appraise patient's emotional needs	1 2 3 4 5
13. Diagnose social problems of patients	1 2 3 4 5
14. Determine patients' need for social services	1 2 3 4 5
15. Detuning type of extended care needed by patients	1 2 3 4 5
16. Recommend treatment for mentally ill patients	1 2 3 4 5
17. Recommend treatment for patients' emotional problems	1 2 3 4 5
18. Strengthen patients' participation in their own care	1 2 3 4 5
19. Help patients overcome personal crises	1 2 3 4 5
20. Help patients to overcome negative feelings about treatment	1 2 3 4 5
21. Encourage patients to follow medical recommendations	1 2 3 4 5
22. Help patients to overcome emotional barriers to discharge	1 2 3 4 5
23. Help patients to overcome emotional barriers to treatment	1 2 3 4 5
24. Provide emotional support to patients	1 2 3 4 5
25. Help patients adjust to separation from families	1 2 3 4 5
26. Help patients adjust to chronic conditions	1 2 3 4 5
27. Help patients adjust to treatment setting	1 2 3 4 5
28. Help patient adjust to illness	1 2 3 4 5
29. Provide psychotherapy to emotionally disturbed patients	1 2 3 4 5
30. Use psychotherapeutic techniques with patients	1 2 3 4 5
31. Prepare family for return of patient	1 2 3 4 5
32. Help patients to improve relations with family	1 2 3 4 5
33. Help families with patients' medical problems	1 2 3 4 5
34. Provide post-hospital employment counseling to patients	1 2 3 4 5
35. Conduct pre-discharge study of homes	1 2 3 4 5

Never or Rarely 1	Seldom 2	Sometimes 3	Often 4	Always or Nearly Always 5

36. Make provisions for patient care in community	1 2 3 4 5
37. Make referrals of patients to community agencies	1 2 3 4 5
38. Provide case consultation to other agencies about patients	1 2 3 4 5
39. Refer families to community agencies	1 2 3 4 5
40. Obtain information on community resources	1 2 3 4 5
41. Act as an advocate in securing community resources for patient	1 2 3 4 5
42. Obtain volunteer resources from community	1 2 3 4 5
43. Interpret hospital services to the community	1 2 3 4 5
44. Interpret hospital services to community agencies	1 2 3 4 5
45. Organize ex-patient groups to improve hospital resources	1 2 3 4 5
46. Orient allied health professionals on psychosocial needs of patients	1 2 3 4 5
47. Give consultation to other professionals on social problems of patients	1 2 3 4 5
48. Orient allied health professionals about social work services	1 2 3 4 5
49. Orient residents about social work services	1 2 3 4 5

Directions: Below is a list of social work activities or functions related to patients care and rehabilitation. You, as a social worker, are being asked to indicate how often you engage in the following activities RELATIVE TO WHEN THE OPPORTUNITY ARISES TO PERFORM THEM. That is, when the need for a particular activity arises, how often do you perform that activity relative to other staff members? Please circle the appropriate number to the right of the task that best represents how often social workers **should be** responsible for carrying out the task. Use the coding system below:

1. NEVER OR RARELY done by social workers (less than 5% of the time)
2. SELDOM done by social workers (about 25% of the time)
3. SOMETIMES done by social workers (about 50% of the time)
4. OFTEN done by social workers (about 75% of the time)
5. ALWAYS OR NEARLY ALWAYS done by social workers (more than 95% of the time)

AS A SOCIAL WORKER:

1. Determine eligibility of patients	1 2 3 4 5
2. Educate patients about hospital services	1 2 3 4 5
3. Help patients obtain medical appliances	1 2 3 4 5
4. Interpret feelings of patients to physicians	1 2 3 4 5
5. Report emotional changes to physicians	1 2 3 4 5
6. Report patients' medical problems to physicians	1 2 3 4 5
7. Report patients' medical symptoms to physicians	1 2 3 4 5
8. Explain physicians' orders to patients	1 2 3 4 5
9. Act as liaison between doctor and patients	1 2 3 4 5
10. Collaborate with other professionals on plan for patients care	1 2 3 4 5

Never or Rarely 1	Seldom 2	Sometimes 3	Often 4	Always or Nearly Always 5

11. Screen patients for psychiatric evaluation	1 2 3 4 5
12. Appraise patient's emotional needs	1 2 3 4 5
13. Diagnose social problems of patients	1 2 3 4 5
14. Determine patients' need for social services	1 2 3 4 5
15. Determine type of extended care needed by patients	1 2 3 4 5
16. Recommend treatment for mentally ill patients	1 2 3 4 5
17. Recommend treatment for patients' emotional problems	1 2 3 4 5
18. Strengthen patients' participation in their own care	1 2 3 4 5
19. Help patients overcome personal crises	1 2 3 4 5
20. Help patients to overcome negative feelings about treatment	1 2 3 4 5
21. Encourage patients to follow medical recommendations	1 2 3 4 5
22. Help patients to overcome emotional barriers to discharge	1 2 3 4 5
23. Help patients to overcome emotional barriers to treatment	1 2 3 4 5
24. Provide emotional support to patients	1 2 3 4 5
25. Help patients adjust to separation from families	1 2 3 4 5
26. Help patients adjust to chronic conditions	1 2 3 4 5
27. Help patients adjust to treatment setting	1 2 3 4 5
28. Help patient adjust to illness	1 2 3 4 5
29. Provide psychotherapy to emotionally disturbed patients	1 2 3 4 5

30. Use psychotherapeutic technique with patients	1 2 3 4 5
31. Prepare family for return of patient	1 2 3 4 5
32. Help patients to improve relations with family	1 2 3 4 5
33. Help families with patients'. Medical problems	1 2 3 4 5
34. Provide post-hospital employment counseling to patients	1 2 3 4 5
35. Conduct pre-discharge study of homes	1 2 3 4 5
36. Make provisions for patient care in community	1 2 3 4 5
37. Make referrals of patients to community agencies	1 2 3 4 5
38. Provide case consultation to other agencies about patients	1 2 3 4 5
39. Refer families to community agencies	1 2 3 4 5
40. Obtain information on community resources	1 2 3 4 5
41. Act as an advocate in securing community resources for patient	1 2 3 4 5
42. Obtain volunteer resources from community	1 2 3 4 5
43. Interpret hospital services to the community	1 2 3 4 5
44. Interpret hospital services to community agencies	1 2 3 4 5
45. Organize ex-patient groups to improve hospital resources	1 2 3 4 5
46. Orient allied health professionals on psychosocial needs of patients	1 2 3 4 5
47. Give consultation to other professionals on social problems of patients	1 2 3 4 5
48. Orient allied health professionals about social work services	1 2 3 4 5
49. Orient residents about social work services	1 2 3 4 5

Part II: Background Information

1. Your age:
    1 - Less than 30
    2 - 31-35
    3 - 36-40
    4 - 41-45
    5 - 46-50
    6 - 51-55
    7 - 56-50
    8 - 60 or over

2. Sex:
    1 - Male
    2 - Female

3. Ethnic Background:
    1 - White non-Hispanic
    2 - Hispanic
    3 - African-American
    4 - Other, please specify:

4. Highest Degree:
    1 - Associate
    2 - Bachelors
    3 - Masters
    4 - Doctorate

5. Years of emergency
*   room experience:*
    1 - Less than 3
    2 - 3-5
    3 - 6-10
    4 - 11-15
    5 - 16 or more

6. Type of control of hos-
*   pital in which yo u are*
*   presently employed:*
    1 - Municipal
    2 - Voluntary not-for-profit

Thank you very much for your help and cooperation.

Cesar M. Garces, MSW
255 Country Road
Medford, New York 11763
Home: (516) 205-0854
Work: (718) 960-1000

I am a doctoral candidate at Yeshiva University, Wurzweiler School of Social Work, preparing to undertake my dissertation research. You have been chosen to participate in this study, under the auspices of Doctor Susan Mason, Professor, Wurzweiler School of Social Work. I am asking for your participation by completing this questionnaire.

The purpose of this study is to explore factors that influence the perceptions that social workers have of their role in the emergency room and the perceptions of other health care professionals of the social workers' role.

The procedure for collecting information is the use of the enclosed questionnaire.

This cover letter explains the study and requests your voluntary participation by completing the questionnaire.

There are no risks to participation. This study will contribute to social policy in its recognition of the need (or lack thereof) to inform and educate health care professionals and administrators about the range of skills and roles that should be performed by social workers in the emergency room. In addition, the research can be used to indicate the extent to which social workers are being fully utilized in emergency rooms.

Your responses will be held confidential and reported only in aggregate form. No participant in the study will be identified in any written or verbal reports. Records may only be inspected by the Human Research Committee on Clinical Investigations (CCI) and the Wurzweiler School of Social Work.

Please complete the questionnaire and returned to the researcher when finished. Results of the study will be made available to anyone who participates.

Zoe H. Parker
4432 Stark Place
Annandale, Virginia 22003
763-323-1772

Cesar Garcia   August 3, 1997
6531 172 St
Fresh Meadow, NY 11365

Dear Cesar,

I'm glad to know my questionnaire is still useful. I am going on vacation so I am writing this now to give you permission to use the questionnaire from my doctoral dissertation for your dissertation study. My only caution is that the scale may be a problem.

and I will look it up when I get back and let you know what the problem is. The questions are old and seemed to work well when I administered it to the various professional groups.

Let me know how it works out. I re-married as you can see by the last name. I will sign both names.

Zoe H. Parker
AKA Zoe Newberson Carrigan

BRONX-LEBANO"
HOSPITAL CENTER

February 24, 1998

Mr. Cesar Garces, CSW
ED Discharge Planning Coordinator
Bronx-Lebanon Hospital Center
1650 Grand Concourse
Bronx, New York

Dear Mr. Garces:

First, I must congratulate you on your commitment to pursing your doctoral degree. I am confident that you will do an excellent job in your research.

I am pleased to grant your request to conduct your research in the Emergency Department.

Good luck in your research!

Sincerely,

Wayne Longmore, M.D., FACEP
Director - Emergency Services

WL:aj

Affiliated with Albert Einstein College of Medicine

1650 Grand Concourse
Bronx, New York 10457
Phone(718)590-1800

BRONX-LEBANO"
HOSPITAL CENTER

February 23, 1998

Mr. Cesar Garces, CSW
ED Discharge Planning Coordinator
Bronx Lebanon Hospital Center
1650 Grand Concourse
Bronx, New York 10457

Dear Mr. Garces,

I am pleased to be able to grant your request to conduct/doctoral research in the Department of Social Work. After discussing your proposal with you I am convinced that your research can only add knowledge and understanding of the role of Social Work.

Please be assured that myself and staff will provide every opportunity available to us to assist you in this endeavor.

I would like to extend my personal congratulations to you for your commitment to this project.

If I can be of further assistance please do not hesitate to contact me.

Sincerely,

Jan S. Jackson St.Hill
Interim Administrator
Social Work/Discharge Planning

Affiliated with Albert Einstein
College of Medicine

1650 Grand Concourse
Bronx, New York 10457
Phone(718)590-1800

374 STOCKHOLM STREET . BROOKLYN, NEW YORK 11237
718 963 7272 VOICE 718 963 7752 FAX

AN AFFILIATE OF THE NEW YORK HOSPITAL · CORNELL MEDICAL CENTER
A MEMBER OF THE NEW YORK AND PRESBYTERIAN HOSPITALS CARE NETWORK

WYCKOFF HEIGHTS MEDICAL CENTER

April 8, 1998

To whom it may concern,

I give Mr. Cesar Garces permission to give questionnaires to the Emergency Room Social Worker
at Wyckoff Heights Medical Center.

Sincerely,

Indira Parmar, ACSW
Director of Social Work

TOTAL P.02

169

WOODHULL MEDICAL CENTER
760 Broadway, Brooklyn, New York 11206-5317

March 16, 1998

Cesar Garces, MSW
6531 172nd Street
Fresh Meadows

Dear Mr. Garces,

      Ms. Robinson and I have reviewed the questionnaires which you have sent me. Your questionnaires are satisfactory for the purpose of being administered to the staff.

I await further instructions from you. If you need to contact me, my phone number is (718) 963-8844/8070

Sincerely,

Douglas Zimmerman, CSW

New York City Health and Hospitals Corporation

March 13, 1998

MONTEFIORE

Mr. Cesar Garces
ED Discharge Planning Coordinator
Bronx Lebanon Hospital Center
1650 Grand Concourse
Bronx, NY 10457

Dear Mr. Garces:

It was my pleasure to meet you and discuss your doctoral research proposal. Your research topic is a valuable one, especially in this era of changing health care and the social work role.

I am pleased to grant you permission on behalf of the social work department to conduct your research in the Department of Social Work and our Emergency Department Social Workers.

If you need further assistance, please call me at (718) 920-4427

Sincerely,

Chinu Chakrabarty, CSW, MSW
Administrative Social Work Manager
Social Work Services Department

313/C98DISK

171

New York City
Health and Hospitals Corporation
Affiliated with
Mt. Sinai School of Medicine

DEPARTMENT OF SOCIAL WORK SERVICES

TO: Whom It May Concern

FROM: Lawrence Cuzzi, DSW
Director, Department of Social Work Services

DATE: March 18, 1998

SUBJECT: Doctoral Dissertation of Cesar Garces

This is to certify that I have given permission to Mr. Garces to give the social workers in my ER a questionnaire that is part of his doctoral dissertation.

79-01 Broadway
Elmhurst, New York 11373
Tel: 718 334-4000

QUEENS HOSPITAL CENTER

New York City Health And Hospitals Corporation
82-68 164th Street, Jamaica, New York 11432
(718) 883-3000

Affiliated with
Mount Sinai School of Medicine

May 15, 1998

Mr. Cesar Carces
65-31 172 St.
Fresh Meadows, N.Y. 11365

Dear Mr. Carces:

As per our conversation, I will be glad to have our
Emergency Room Social Worker complete the questionnaire
you are developing.

However, I wish to review this instrument before sub-
mission to my staff.

Sincerely,

Robert Ferrer, Director
Social Work Services

RF:jac

METROPOLITAN HOSPITAL CENTER
1901 First Avenue / 97th Street, New York, NY 10029

Jeanne M. Atkatz, D.S.W.
Director
Social Work
Tel: (212) 423-7051/7063 Fax: (212) 423-6388

TO: Whom It May Concern

FROM: Dr. Jeanne M. Atkatz, DSW
           Director of Social Work Department

SUBJECT: Doctoral Dissertation of Cesar Garces

DATE: March 20, 1998

This is to certify that I have given permission to Mr. Garces to
give the social workers in my Emergency Room a Questionnaire
that is part of his Doctoral Dissertation.

WOODHULL MEDICAL AND MENTAL HEALTH CENTER
760 Broadway, Brooklyn, New York 11206

Fernando A. Jara, M.D.
Director
Emergency Medicine Department
(718) 963-5735

March 10, 1995

To whom it may concern.

Cecar Garces is given by my permission to interview Woodhull Hospital Emergency Room physicians.

Thank you

[signature]

LINCOLN

LINCOLN MEDICAL AND MENTAL HEALTH CENTER
234 EUGENIO MARIA DE HOSTOS BLVD (149TH STREET)
THE BRONX, NEW YORK 10451 • 718-579-5000

February 26, 1998

TO WHOM IT MAY CONCERN:

Cesar Garces, MSW was granted permission to interview Emergency Department Staff outside the Emergency Department on February 27, 1998. Mr. Garces is doing research at the Wurzweiler School of Social Work, Yeshiva University.   His research deals with physicians and nurses perception of social workers functional role.

I feel that his research is beneficial to the medical community and I'm sure that our staff will be more than happy to assist him.

Sincerely,

Gregory L. Boris, DO
Associate Director/
Adult Emergency Dept.

GLB:ys

c: File

LINCOLN

LINCOLN MEDICAL AND MENTAL HEALTH CENTER
234 EL GENIO MARIA DE BOSTOS BLVD. (149TH STREET)
THE BRONX, NEW YORK 10451 • 718-579-5000

April 3, 1998

To Whom It May Concern:

Cesar Garces, MSW is granted permission to conduct his Doctoral Survey on "Social Work Activities in the Emergency Department." The surveys will be given to Ms. Dorothy Grant, CSW, Associate Director of Social Work Services for distribution to the Emergency Department Social Work staff.

The survey was reviewed by me and it should only take a few minutes to complete. It is understood that no findings will report on individual workers or Lincoln Medical and Mental Health Center.

Sincerely,

Charles Cohen, CSW, ACSW
AED Patient Care Management

cc: Lilliam Barrios-Paoli
       Albion Fitzgerald
       Dorothy Grant

c:\office\charlie\socialwk\docstud.498

NYU
Medical
Center

Social Work Department
400 East 34th Street, New York, NY 10016
Cable Address: NYUMEDIC

(212) 263-

3/1/98

To whom it may concern:

Mr. Cesar Garces has my permission to interview Tisch Hospital Emergency Room Social
Workers in conjunction with his doctoral dissertation.

E. Chachkes /m. Piven
Esther Chachkes
Social Work Director

www.ingramcontent.com/pod-product-compliance
Lightning Source LLC
Chambersburg PA
CBHW021631120626
46545CB00002B/496